The Stations Of The Cross:
Think Upon These Things

By Earl Clinton Williams, Jr.

ISBN: **1467980641**
ISBN-13: **978-1467980647**

<u>Dedication</u>

This book is dedicated to the Holy Trinity and to all of those whose stories and wisdom that you will read

CONTENTS

Acknowledgments

There are some very special people that I would like to thank when it comes to this book and my life. In different ways they have help me in some way in making me the person that I am. I would also like to thank some of the people for being who they are as they have made a difference in my life. If it seems like I have forgotten your name, it wasn't on purpose.

My Parents, Earl & Irene Williams
My Sister, Karen Williams
My Nephews, Kenneth & Faheem Williams
My Grandparents, May they Rest In Peace
All of my Aunts, Uncles and Cousins
My Godparents Jesse Cooke, Inez Cooke, Isaac Hamm, Ysadore Hamm
My Childhood Friends
The Episcopal Diocese Of Pennsylvania
The Episcopal Diocese of California
The Society Of Friends, also known as The Quakers
The Members of Calvary Episcopal Church, Philadelphia, Pa.
The Members of The House Of Prayer Episcopal Church, Philadelphia, Pa.
The Members of Grace Epiphany Episcopal Church, Philadelphia, Pa.
The Members of St. Cuthbert's Episcopal Church, Oakland, Ca.
The Members of St. James The Greater Episcopal Church, Oakland, Ca.
Lorielle New
Jananie Priyaa
Nancy Duranteau
The Rev. John & Milene Rawlinson
The Rt. Rev. Marc Handley Andrus, Bishop of the Episcopal Diocese Of California
Gerald Learn
Alice Rockwell
The Experience Project
The Staff Of The Oakland Public Libraries

The History of
The Stations Of The Cross*

The Stations of the Cross originated in pilgrimages to Jerusalem. A desire to reproduce the holy places in other lands seems to have manifested itself at quite an early date. At the monastery of Santo Stefano at Bologna a group of connected chapels was constructed as early as the 5th century, by St. Petronius, Bishop of Bologna, which was intended to represent the more important shrines of Jerusalem, and in consequence, this monastery became familiarly known as "Hierusalem." These may perhaps be regarded as the germ from which the Stations afterward developed, though it is tolerably certain that nothing that we have before about the 15th century can strictly be called a Way of the Cross in the modern sense. Although several travelers who visited the Holy Land during the twelfth, thirteenth, and 14th centuries (e.g. Riccoldo da Monte di Croce,Burchard of Mount Sion, James of Verona),mention a "Via Sacra," i.e., a settled route along which pilgrims were conducted, there is nothing in their accounts to identify this with the Way of the Cross, as we understand it.The devotion of the Via Dolorosa, for which there have been a number of variant routes in Jerusalem, was probably developed by the Franciscans after they were granted administration of the Christian holy places in Jerusalem in 1342.

The earliest use of the word "stations," as applied to the accustomed halting-places in the Via Sacra at Jerusalem, occurs in the narrative of an English pilgrim, William Wey, who visited the Holy Land in the mid-15th century, and described pilgrims following the footsteps of Christ to the cross. In 1521 a book called Geystlich Strass was printed with illustrations of the stations in the Holy Land.

During the 15th and 16th centuries the Franciscans began to build a series of outdoor shrines in Europe to duplicate their counterparts in the Holy Land. The number of stations varied between eleven and thirty. In 1686, in answer to their petition, Pope Innocent XI granted to the Franciscans the right to erect stations within their churches. In 1731, Pope Clement XII extended to all churches the right to have the stations, provided that a Franciscan father erected them, with the consent of the local bishop. At the same time the number was fixed at fourteen. In 1857, the bishops of England were allowed to erect the stations by themselves, without the intervention of a Franciscan priest, and in 1862 this right was extended to bishops throughout the church.

*This history comes from Wikipedia and is the best that I think that I can find. I am not claiming that it is 100% correct as many people will state many different histories to the origin of this Christian practice. My personal belief is that it got started when things actually occurred in the last few days of Jesus Christ.

About This Book And
How The Stations Are Done

Over the years I had done The Stations Of The Cross not only during the Lenten season, but throughout the year, as I believe that we should not just hear the story of Christ's Passion during that time of year, but at all times. One day I wanted to do it at home, but I didn't have a copy of it to use, so I did a search on the Internet where I came across a number of different versions surrounding different themes. I brought the idea to the congregation that I am in and that we do the Stations every Friday during Lent, with the service on Good Friday being the traditional service. It was agreed to give it a try that year. Even though the attendance wasn't that great, for those who did come (which included people who were not members of the congregation,) the using of the themes was well received.

During the year after that, I looked for other themes to us, then the idea of putting one together dealing with Racism occurred to me. I had been involved in a committee that was dealing with Racism a few years earlier where I had put a type of Stations Of the Cross together, so I took some of those stories that I had collected, along with some new ones, and put it into a traditional format. We used it the next year, and so it began. I plan to continue to put together more surrounding other topics.

The way that things are done in with these stations is that a stand is placed in front of the congregation. With each Station one or more people come from the pews to read each station. Nobody is to do stations back-to-back, nor is ordination required to do a Station.

With some of the Stations after the last one is done there are either prayers and/or a speech concerning the topic. I strongly suggest that a youth lead either the prayers and/or read the speech. My belief is that if we really want for youth to be in our churches, then we must get them involved in different aspects of the service outside of the traditional areas like being in the choir and/or acolyte. When they feel as though they are apart of the service, they feel important.

What could also be done is to insert your own stories in place of the stories included. Ask within your congregation for people to write down their stories concerning the topics. Even though you may think that the people will not have any personal stories to tell, you might be surprised at how many stories emerge that you don't know about. Don't ask for the stories that people heard about, but their personal stories.

Also don't feel as though you would need to use ALL of the different themed Stations in this book, just the one(s) that you feel that you need...

About the Artwork & Photography

Much of the artwork and photographs in this book came from three sources. The photograph on the cover is a photo that I took as a flight that I was on was landing at the Oakland International Airport on December 31, 2010 during the evening. Normally I sit on the other side of the plane, but for some reason I choose to sit on the opposite site. I guess is that it is what the Holy Trinity wanted for me to do. We had been told to turn off all of our electronic stuff, but when I saw the view outside of the plane, I just knew that I had to take a picture.

The artwork with the halos is from the Icon Series that actress and artist Lorielle New did. I had met her through a daily Internet talk show that she does several years ago, and actually got to meet her in person while I was on a trip to Los Angeles in August, 2010. She is a wonderful person, a wonderful actress and a wonderful painter. You can check out and buy some of her original works on her website www.loriellenew.com

A few of the artwork and photographs were done be a young lady in Singapore named Jananie Priyaa. I met her online at a video chat site and became very fond of her works. I have never met her in person, but have found her to be a very intelligent young lady.

Other artwork and photographs are things that I found in the public domain on the Internet.

Earl & Lorielle, August 2011

Stations Of The Cross

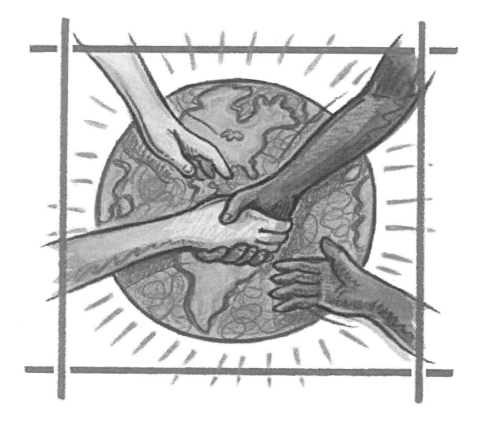

Let's Talk About Race

By Earl Clinton Williams, Jr.

Acclamations

What you are about to read and experience will hopefully make you think about Race and Racism and how you can help to not only help the world to become a place where this subject will become a thing of the past, but it will hopefully help you into making better choices in the way that you treat others of different colors, nationalities, ethnic groups, and much more in a better way. Hopefully this will make you realize that no matter how much you may deny that you are a racist, you will realize that EVERYBODY has a bit of it in them. Many people look and think that it's those who are in such groups as the KKK and Nazis that are racist, but even those who think that they are on the total opposite end of that kind of thinking do racist things themselves.

I would like to give big thanks to my friends and family, the people on The Experience Project (www.experienceproject.com) and others who's stories that are within these pages. I would like to give a special thanks to damili ayo, one of my favorite authors and one of the best social justice advocates that this world has toward working for equality for all. I would like to give thanks to ALL that have died fighting for equality for all. most importantly I would like to thank my parents, sister, nephews, grandparent, the Quakers, The Episcopal Church, the people of Grace Epiphany Episcopal Church in Philadelphia, Pa. and others who have helped me to understand that there is more to people than the color of their skin.

I would also like to give thanks to the Holy Trinity in guiding me through the process of putting this together. I only hope and pray that this is an instrument that will help this world become a better place.

Station 1: Jesus in the Garden of Gethsemane

-

Leader: We adore you, oh Christ, and we bless you.
All: **Because by your holy cross you have redeemed the world.**

Reading:

Then Jesus came with them to a place called Gethsemane, and he said to his disciples, "Sit here while I go over there and pray." He took along Peter and the two sons of Zebedee, and began to feel sorrow and distress. Then he said to them, "My soul is sorrowful even to death. Remain here and keep watch with me." He advanced a little and fell prostrate in prayer, saying, "My Father, if it is possible, let this cup pass from me; yet, not as I will, but as you will." When he returned to his disciples he found them asleep. He said to Peter, "So you could not keep watch with me for one hour? Watch and pray that you may not undergo the test. The spirit is willing, but the flesh is weak."
Matthew 25:36-41

Moment of Silence

Story:

"Silence at the airport"

A colleague went to the Viennese Airport and got himself a "Schnitzel" at the local restaurant. If you know the airport, there is one restaurant where you need to get your meal from the counter. He put the Schnitzel on a table, and realized he forgot the fork and knife. He went back to the counter, got his instruments and went back to the table. At the table, an African young man sat and ate his Schnitzel. With a mumbled "What the heck?" he sat down, staring at the young man eating his meal. Knowing his flight would leave really soon, he just calmed down, without saying a word, and ate too. The same Schnitzel. After the Schnitzel was gone, the stranger got up and got a dessert. He put it on the table and moved it into the middle. Both ate the dessert. Without saying a word.

Now, the dessert was eaten, and the stranger got up and left. The colleague got up as well, and then realized that he didn't sit down at his table. His Schnitzel was untouched and lonely at a table in the other corner. He ate the Schnitzel and Dessert of the stranger.

Moment of Silence

All: Jesus our friend and brother, through your life and your journey to the cross, your death and resurrection, you have shown us how to live in love. May we always follow your example, living in redemption, living a life of compassion, in the search for peace through justice for all your people.

Station 2: Jesus, Betrayed by Judas, is Arrested

Leader: We adore you, oh Christ, and we bless you.
All: **Because by your holy cross you have redeemed the world.**

Reading:

Then, while [Jesus] was still speaking, Judas, one of the Twelve, arrived, accompanied by a crowd with swords and clubs, who had come from the chief priests, the scribes, and the elders. His betrayer had arranged a signal with them, saying, "the man I shall kiss is the one; arrest him and lead him away securely." He came and immediately went over to him and said, "Rabbi." And he kissed him. At this they laid hands on him and arrested him.
Mark 14: 43-46

Moment of Silence

Story:

I used to work at the Mall of America. I worked at a retail store that sold Minnesota products-t-shirts, magnets, etc. A recurring event began to happen that I wasn't prepared for: I would have African American women repeatedly approach me, and be mean (and I mean EVIL!), saying that 'my people' (college-age blonds, I guess) were 'stealing' their men, and therefore trying to destroy any hope for the continuation of their ethnic heritage. I wasn't married at the time, but I was dating my husband--who is WAY white, so I didn't see why they were mad at me. I have dated black guys, and there was never any problem or race issue-at all. They were just like any other boyfriend, it seemed. This happened all the time, mostly to blond girls. And it was always the same women that would cause the trouble. (Apparently a case of 'too much free time on their hands'.) When it escalated to harassing levels, the security would always ask them to behave properly or leave the property. This of course didn't help matters because then it was a 'we (black women) were kicked out of a public place for picking on the white girls'. Then they would call the local news stations, to say they had been victims of racism, and you can see were it all goes wrong at this point.

So, whose 'fault' is it? The white girl from a small town who is just trying not to irritate anyone or cause trouble? Or the black girl who would follow her around and threaten her? I don't know. It seemed to me, that these particular women were causing trouble, and it doesn't resemble any of the African American women I have met since, so I would tend to blame those exact women. But, from the other side maybe it would seem like racism-but why was it my fault? Me because I'm white? To tell the truth, I'm a big chicken, and don't like being picked on by anyone-I don't care what their race is!!! "

Moment of Silence

All: Jesus our friend and brother, through your life and your journey to the cross, your death and resurrection, you have shown us how to live in love. May we always follow your example, living in redemption, living a life of compassion, in the search for peace through justice for all your people.

Station 3: Jesus is Condemned by the Sanhedrin

Leader: We adore you, oh Christ, and we bless you.
All: **Because by your holy cross you have redeemed the world.**

Reading:

When day came the council of elders of the people met, both chief priests and scribes, and they brought him before their Sanhedrin. They said, "If you are the Messiah, tell us," but he replied to them, "If I tell you, you will not believe, and if I question, you will not respond. But from this time on the Son of Man will be seated at the right hand of the power of God." They all asked, "Are you then the Son of God?" He replied to them, "You say that I am." Then they said, "What further need have we for testimony? We have heard it from his own mouth."
Luke 22: 66-71

Moment of Silence

Story:

Scene took place on a British Airways flight between Johannesburg and London.

A White woman, about 50 years old, was seated next to a black man. Obviously disturbed by this, she called the air Hostess. "Madam, what is the matter," the hostess asked. "You obviously do not see it then?"she responded. "You placed me next to a black man. I do not agree to sit next to someone from such a repugnant group. Give me an alternative seat." "Be calm please," the hostess replied. "Almost all the places on this flight are taken. I will go to see if another place is available."

The Hostess went away and then came back a few minutes later. "Madam, just as I thought, there are no other available seats in the economy class. I spoke to the captain and he informed me that there is a seat in the business class. All the same, we still have one place in the first class." Before the woman could say anything, the hostess continued: "It is not usual for our company to permit someone from the economy class to sit in the first class. However, given the circumstances, the captain feels that it would be scandalous to make someone sit next to someone so disgusting."

She turned to the black guy, and said, "Therefore, Sir, if you would like to, please collect your hand luggage, a seat awaits you in first class."At that moment, the other passengers who were shocked by what they had just witnessed stood up and applauded.

Moment of Silence

All: Jesus our friend and brother, through your life and your journey to the cross, your death and resurrection, you have shown us how to live in love. May we always follow your example, living in redemption, living a life of compassion, in the search for peace through justice for all your people.

Station 4: Jesus is Denied by Peter

Leader: We adore you, oh Christ, and we bless you.
All: **Because by your holy cross you have redeemed the world.**

Reading:

Now Peter was sitting outside in the courtyard. One of the maids came over to him and said, "You too were with Jesus the Galilean." But he denied it in front of everyone, saying, "I do not know what you are talking about!" As he went out to the gate, another girl saw him and said to those who were there, "This man was with Jesus the Nazorean." Again he denied it with an oath, "I do not know the man!" A little later the bystanders came over and said to Peter, "Surely you too are one of them; even your speech gives you away." At that he began to curse and to swear, "I do not know the man." And immediately a cock crowed. Then Peter remembered the word that Jesus had spoken: "Before the cock crows you will deny me three times." He went out and began to weep bitterly.
Matthew 26: 69-75

Moment of Silence

Story:

I went into Walgreens to pick up somethings...at the checkout counter, the cashier looks at me (pauses) and asks "are you Italian?" no I am not. "Indian?" no...clearly he isn't going to give up so I tell him my ethnicity. His response? "wow you speak really great English for being an immigrant" my response: " I am American, I was born here." (shocker!) his reply: "oh....well, still...your English is still great for having parents who are immigrants." my reply: "I am 4th generation...my grandfather fought in the Korean war." his reply: "oh..." What I really wanted to tell this guy was "Hey, your English is suburb- especially since you are of African origin and had to have immigrated from some little village in some country on the African continent." but then I would be a racist bigot. what is an American anyway? Last I checked the majority of the American population are decedents of immigrants. just because I have dark hair eyes and light olive skin I can't speak English? Do people not realize that English is spoken and taught in other countries besides America, the UK and Australia? Skin color does not change your citizenship, and surprisingly enough, "white" is not an origin. everyone came from somewhere and here is the big shocker... we are all citizens of the planet earth and we are all human, regardless of complexion. why is this such a hard concept to grasp?

Moment of Silence

All: Jesus our friend and brother, through your life and your journey to the cross, your death and resurrection, you have shown us how to live in love. May we always follow your example, living in redemption, living a life of compassion, in the search for peace through justice for all your people.

Station 5: Jesus is Judged by Pilate

Leader: We adore you, oh Christ, and we bless you.
All: **Because by your holy cross you have redeemed the world.**

Reading:

The chief priests with the elders and the scribes, that is, the whole Sanhedrin, held a council. They bound Jesus, led him away, and handed him over to Pilate. Pilate questioned him, "Are you the king of the Jews?" He said to him in reply, "You say so." The chief priests accused him of many things. Again Pilate questioned him, "Have you no answer? See how many things they accuse you of." Jesus gave him no further answer, so that Pilate was amazed.... Pilate, wishing to satisfy the crowd, released Barrabas... [and] handed [Jesus] over to be crucified.
Mark 15: 1-5, 15

Moment of Silence

Story:

Being Black is hard enough, as the people in the world see me for my color first, but it is even hard in the church. I was on a commission in a diocese where an event was being planned. One thing that was wanted for this event was for each of the ethnic groups to something to be part of the event. As we went through this planning, and those of other races brought forth things, I wondered what could come from the Black community as it seemed that because of history we have become "assimilated" into society and the church. The planning was done, then I realized what we do have something to offer, that being music. I brought it up and said that all of the music will be from the Afro-Anglican community. The others were happy with this idea, and I was asked about one song to use, but another song had popped into my mind, and I said what it was. Suddenly the others in the group started coming up and inserting songs from other ethnic groups. All that I could do was to 'throw my hands up'; as I knew that I would hear excuses as to why we must include these other songs from other cultures and ethnic groups.

The day of the event comes, and we have a guest facilitator. We started with the only African-American song, and after we sang it, the facilitator criticized the song once he came up to the podium. At the end of the day I hear people talking about how great the other songs that we sang we, but nobody said anything about the one song that was criticized.

I wonder to this day what we Blacks in this diocese need to do so that we can feel as though we have brought something to the table.

Moment of Silence

All: Jesus our friend and brother, through your life and your journey to the cross, your death and resurrection, you have shown us how to live in love. May we always follow your example, living in redemption, living a life of compassion, in the search for peace through justice for all your people.

Station 6: Jesus is Scourged and Crowned with Thorns

Leader: We adore you, oh Christ, and we bless you.
All: **Because by your holy cross you have redeemed the world.**

Reading:

Then Pilate took Jesus and had him scourged. And the soldiers wove a crown out of thorns and placed it on his head, and clothed him in a purple cloak, and they came to him and said,"Hail, King of the Jews!" And they struck him repeatedly.

John 19: 1-3

Moment of Silence

Story:

You know how your parents and teachers and everyone always tells you that it's the insides that count? I believed that wholeheartedly until 7th grade.

I was just starting to 'like' girls. my best friend (who was white) had this group of girls he had met somewhere- he would call them variously and talk to them. he gave them my number too. We would call each other and talk about nothing for hours- just being Jr. High kids. My buddy even met up with some of them at the mall and hung out.
At some point we decided we would all meet and see a movie. My buddy and I waited in front until the movie had already started, and then finally gave up and went inside.

The girls never called me again, and were never around when I called them. Eventually my buddy admitted that he had seen them at the movies, but they wouldn't come over when they saw I was black. He said they were shocked because I didn't 'sound black' on the phone...

Moment of Silence

All: Jesus our friend and brother, through your life and your journey to the cross, your death and resurrection, you have shown us how to live in love. May we always follow your example, living in redemption, living a life of compassion, in the search for peace through justice for all your people.

Station 7: Jesus Bears the Cross

Leader: We adore you, oh Christ, and we bless you.
All: **Because by your holy cross you have redeemed the world.**

Reading:

When the chief priests and the guards saw [Jesus] they cried out, "Crucify him, crucify him!" Pilate said to them, "Take him yourselves and crucify him. I find no guilt in him." ... They cried out, "Take him away, take him away! Crucify him!" Pilate said to them, "Shall I crucify your king?" The chief priests answered, "We have no king but Caesar." Then he handed him over to them to be crucified. So they took Jesus, and carrying the cross himself he went out to what is called the Place of the Skull, in Hebrew, Golgotha. John 19: 6, 15-17

Moment of Silence

Story:

The first time was when I was in 6th grade and I was quite the little track star. Therefore, my boyfriend was an athlete, track star, as well. He, like me, was usually in 1st place for just about every event. One day my oldest brother made a comment about black people and I called him out on it, as much as a 6th grader can. And he then warned me that if I ever bring home a black guy that he will beat the crap out of both of us.

Flash to my Freshman year in high school. Another boyfriend, of course, and he happened to be of mixed race, Black and Filipino. We had plans to go to a party together and he was going to pick me up. My mother was out and my grandparents were visiting. When he knocked on the door, my grandmother opened it and asked what he wanted. He told he he was there to pick me up and she replied that he must be mistaken, that I was going out with a boyfriend of mine. He assured her that he was, in fact, that boyfriend. She told him hell no and closed the door in his face. She forbid me from doing anything that night, although my mother had already told me it was OK. But my grandfather, who was ultimately cool, told me to go to my room (and then followed me there, whispering to me that I should just go out the window...)

I was raised in the South, in a staunchly conservative, religious, Republican family. They've never understood me and I have never understood them. But I can tell you this ~ the ugly cycle of racism, in my family, stops with me. My child will never be like them.

Moment of Silence

All: Jesus our friend and brother, through your life and your journey to the cross, your death and resurrection, you have shown us how to live in love. May we always follow your example, living in redemption, living a life of compassion, in the search for peace through justice for all your people.

Station 8: Jesus is Helped by Simon the Cyrenian to Carry the Cross

Leader: We adore you, oh Christ, and we bless you.
All: **Because by your holy cross you have redeemed the world.**

Reading:

They pressed into service a passer-by, Simon, a Cyrenian, who was coming in from the country, the father of Alexander and Rufus, to carry his cross.
Mark 15: 21

Moment of Silence

Story:

When I was dating one of my boyfriends from high school I always had to drive. If he drove there had to have been at least a 90% chance we would get pulled over. Usually nothing was done wrong and the cop would make up some stupid reason for pulling us over and then give him a warning (tire looks low on air, didn't put the turning signal on early enough, etc).

One time we had parked somewhere secluded. We hadn't been there very long when a cop came out of no where and banged on the window. He practically dragged me out of the car then asked me if I was being raped. I told him no, this is my boyfriend. Then he asked me if it was my car we were in and I told him no. Then he said that he would give me a ride home. I asked why, was I under arrest or something and he told me that I shouldn't be with this kind of people and that I should think about the shame my family would feel if I was with a black man. I've never been good at coming up with words on the spot so I swung at him. I missed and he slammed me up against the side of his car. My boyfriend (who was in his car still) asked what was going on and the cop told him to stay in the car. He patted me down and told me under his breath that he was just trying to help and if I wanted to be a ***** I could but not in his town. He let me go back to the car and then he told my boyfriend that if he ever saw either of us parked out here again he would arrest us both.

Moment of Silence

All: Jesus our friend and brother, through your life and your journey to the cross, your death and resurrection, you have shown us how to live in love. May we always follow your example, living in redemption, living a life of compassion, in the search for peace through justice for all your people.

Station 9: Jesus Meets the Women of Jerusalem

Leader: We adore you, oh Christ, and we bless you.
All: **Because by your holy cross you have redeemed the world.**

Reading:

A large crowd of people followed Jesus, including many women who mourned and lamented him. Jesus turned to them and said, "Daughters of Jerusalem, do not weep for me; weep instead for yourselves and for your children, for indeed, the days are coming when people will say, 'Blessed are the barren, the wombs that never bore and the breasts that never nursed.' At that time, people will say to the mountains, 'Fall upon us!' and to the hills, 'Cover us!' for if these things are done when the wood is green what will happen when it is dry?"
Luke 23: 27-31

Moment of Silence

Story:

It amazes me that we talk about wanting to live in a world where we all are treated as equals regardless of race, color, sex, age, sexuality and many other thing, but we keep using terms that do nothing but remind us of our difference and divide us.

Over the past 20 years or so, I have heard this term "Third World" being used. I have found this term to be very racist, classist and not of any help in creating a world that we are all equals. I often ask people who use the term as to where these other worlds are that are supporting human life, as I don't recall NASA or any other space agency having passenger services to these places.

I wish that people would really think about the term and how much it is against the dream of Rev. Dr. Marting Luther King, Jr. and other great leaders pass and present. What makes our society much better than others? "But the term is about Industrialized and non- industrialized nations and places...," I can hear people saying. Interesting. Could someone please explain to me then how a "world" that is destroying the planet, fighting wars, and so forth is better than a "world" that is living and using the resources that it really needs to survive with very little impact on the planet?

The first time that I heard this term used, it was used against me by someone who was an outright racist. I think that she thought that it would be OK for her to use that term, because if she used "nigger" she would of found herself in deep trouble. Now I really wouldn't of said anything if she went the other way, because I knew that the other Blacks that were around would beat the crap out of her. She did get cussed out by them for what she said by them, but it would have been worse for her if she had gone the other way.

A few years later, I heard the term being used on television. I found this troubling, and I began to think. Why would people use should a offensive word? What makes us better than someone else because of what our country has? Are other places feeling as though they have been insulted because of this term? I had so many questions running through my mind about this, and I knew that if I were to ask people what they meant by the term, and my feelings as to the term, they wouldn't stop.

Will we ever come to a point where we don't see each other as a color, but only a race, where that race will be the Human Race? Until the time in which we all just look and think of this as One World, I don't think that we can truly come together to honor and respect the planet that we live on.

Moment of Silence

All: Jesus our friend and brother, through your life and your journey to the cross, your death and resurrection, you have shown us how to live in love. May we always follow your example, living in redemption, living a life of compassion, in the search for peace through justice for all your people.

Station 10: Jesus is Crucified

Leader: We adore you, oh Christ, and we bless you.
All: **Because by your holy cross you have redeemed the world.**

Reading:

When they came to the place called the Skull, they crucified him and the criminals there, one on his right, the other on his left. [Then Jesus said, "Father, forgive them, they know not what they do."]
Luke 23: 33-34

Moment of Silence

Story:

I had been having a wonderful day up until that point. It was my birthday and my best friend had treated me to a great spa day. I felt great. She decided to take me shopping as well. (I should probably mention that my friend and I are African-Americans) I saw a dress in a window and decided to go in. I had just come from school earlier that morning before meeting up with my friend and had my bag slung over my shoulder.

As soon as I stepped in, a group of white salespeople surrounded me and a black security guard as well. Lots of other people had come in right behind me, all of them white, and many of them had bags, bulky purses and purchases from other stores. No one stopped them.

I offered to let them check my bag, but the salesgirl declined and asked angrily "What do you want?" I told her "to shop of course." Everyone was looking at both my friend and I as if we had committed a crime. Everyone in the store was staring and I was embarrassed. The security guard was looking at me evilly. That's what hurt the most. I would think a fellow African-American would understand racism more than anyone else. But that's what happens sometimes. Sometimes we are our own worst enemies.

Anyway, my friend got really angry and demanded to speak to a manager and asked why we were being detained. Then the salespeople got nervous. Well, my friend was determined not to let it get us down and grabbed my hand and pulled me past them. The salespeople followed us around the entire time. I couldn't even move without bumping into one of them.

At that point, I didn't even want to get anything from that store. I felt tainted. Here I was, a law abiding citizen, going to college, supposedly doing everything right and I was still treated like a common criminal before even stepping into the store. We looked around for a minute, but I just couldn't bring myself to get anything there. We finally left and went to another store. It was surprising that this happened at a very popular and recognizable store. I was so hurt, I could never bring myself to shop there.

Unfortunately, this is tip of the iceberg as far as racist things I've experienced. I have since learned some hard truths. No matter how well behaved, well coiffed, moneyed, educated and nice you are, many times, it doesn't matter. Some people will only judge you by the attributes they perceive to be connected to your skin color.

Moment of Silence

All: Jesus our friend and brother, through your life and your journey to the cross, your death and resurrection, you have shown us how to live in love. May we always follow your example, living in redemption, living a life of compassion, in the search for peace through justice for all your people.

Station 11: Jesus Promises His Kingdom to the Good Thief

Leader: We adore you, oh Christ, and we bless you.
All: **Because by your holy cross you have redeemed the world.**

Reading:

Now one of the criminals hanging there reviled Jesus, saying, "Are you not the Messiah? Save yourself and us." The other, however, rebuking him, said in reply, "Have you no fear of God, for you are subject to the same condemnation? And indeed, we have been condemned justly, for the sentence we received corresponds to our crimes, but this man has done nothing criminal." Then he said, "Jesus, remember me when you come into your kingdom." He replied to him, "Amen, I say to you, today you will be with me in Paradise."
Luke 23: 39-43

Moment of Silence

Story:

My skin color is black, but I'm human. In my mind there's no such thing as the white, black, Latino, Chinese, etc. race. There is one race for human beings, and that is HUMAN -- THE HUMAN RACE. I don't get the big deal between distinguishing people of sorts when describing someone. Maybe the media has taken it into effect, or people of the old days not getting used to the contemporary days. I overheard an old lady in a grocery story one day talking to another old lady saying, "this 'black' guy was making a lot of commotion." Why say "black guy," "white guy," "Latino guy," or any color-associated guy reference. Why not say guy? Why distinguish between? There's one race, and it's human, baby.

Moment of Silence

All: Jesus our friend and brother, through your life and your journey to the cross, your death and resurrection, you have shown us how to live in love. May we always follow your example, living in redemption, living a life of compassion, in the search for peace through justice for all your people.

Station 12: Jesus Speaks to His Mother and the Disciple

Leader: We adore you, oh Christ, and we bless you.
All: **Because by your holy cross you have redeemed the world.**

Reading:

Standing by the cross of Jesus were his mother and his mother's sister, Mary the wife of Clopas, and Mary of Magdala. When Jesus saw his mother and the disciple there whom he loved, he said to his mother, "Woman, behold, your son." Then he said to the disciple, "Behold, your mother." And from that hour the disciple took her into his home.
John 19: 25-27

Moment of Silence

Story:

Getting past the stereotypes is hard enough. Nevertheless I enjoy living in the culture. I enjoy my kinky hair and the endless things that I can do with it. I enjoy my full lips and my Carmel skin. I enjoy knowing how to switch from professional to "girlfriend" when appropriate. It is uncomfortable at times when I sit in a classroom and there is only one other black person. But really after a while (after proving myself) I am included and treated as if I had positive input in the class.

I just wish that I didn't have to work so hard at trying to get my non black classmates to get past the stereotypes.

Moment of Silence

All: Jesus our friend and brother, through your life and your journey to the cross, your death and resurrection, you have shown us how to live in love. May we always follow your example, living in redemption, living a life of compassion, in the search for peace through justice for all your people.

Station 13: Jesus Dies on the Cross

Leader: We adore you, oh Christ, and we bless you.
All: **Because by your holy cross you have redeemed the world.**

Reading:

It was now about noon and darkness came over the whole land until three in the afternoon because of an eclipse of the sun. Then the veil of the temple was torn down the middle. Jesus cried out in a loud voice, "Father, into your hands I commend my spirit"; and when he had said this he breathed his last.
Luke 23: 44-46

Moment of Silence

Story:

Here's a little example... A - A friend's brother B- Me

A: What College are you attending?

B: U-Chicago

A: *Surprised look* Really? *laughs* Affirmative action right?

B: No, not at all. U-Chicago is known to be competitive and they are not big supporters of affirmative action from what my counselor tells me & if you were to....

A:*Cuts me Off* Ha, you sure. I mean, how else would a black person get into a phenomenal school like the University of Chicago? I mean, yeah, I hear you're smart but not that smart. Let me guess? You ditched your ghetto African talk and prepped it up for the interview and you .....

He's cut off by his sister

Unbelievable & sad.

I can only imagine what he would have said if he were to continue.

P.S. I noticed in one story someone commented and said something like, "Sweetie, you call that racism..." or something along those lines.

I'm a firm believer in the fact that Racism is Racism. Regardless of if you are called a name, physically hurt...etc. Pain is pain & when one is effected negatively as a result of racism it's not your role to judge how bad it is. Yes, sure, lecture them and prepare them for what may come and what has happened, but try to avoid being smug. =)

We're here to share experiences. Not bash each other and cry "My situation was worse!"

Moment of Silence

All: Jesus our friend and brother, through your life and your journey to the cross, your death and resurrection, you have shown us how to live in love. May we always follow your example, living in redemption, living a life of compassion, in the search for peace through justice for all your people.

Station 14: Jesus is Placed in the Tomb

Leader: We adore you, oh Christ, and we bless you.
All: **Because by your holy cross you have redeemed the world.**

Reading:

When it was evening, there came a rich man from Arimathea named Joseph, who was himself a disciple of Jesus. He went to Pilate and asked for the body of Jesus; then Pilate ordered it to be handed over. Taking the body, Joseph wrapped it [in] clean linen and laid it in his new tomb that he had hewn in the rock. Then he rolled a huge stone across the entrance to the tomb and departed.
Matthew 27: 57-60

Moment of Silence

Story:

I must've been around 8 years old or so, and we lived in this compound which mainly consisted of families of foreigners, who were there for work or who newly settled in the country.

I had a number of friends from England, Greece and Portugal within the compound, and I had a bunch of Zimbabwean friends who lived in nearby buildings.

One of my black Zimbabwean friends belonged to a poor family that lived in a little house made of tin, not too far from the compound we lived in.

I really liked him and enjoyed playing with him a lot. I'd go around with other Zimbabwean friends sometimes and other times on my own, and we'd go out and play all kinds of games; Almost anything is enjoyable when you're a kid.

Our friendship grew, and all was great until his father knew about it and he started telling his son not to play with me because I was white.

I thought that was unfair, and I didn't understand why such a thing could matter at all, so I didn't give up and I kept sneaking over to my friend's place to take him out to play.

His father caught me while sneaking in a number of times and started running after me with a stick, trying to scare me away from coming back to play with his son, but I'd just outrun him, jump over fences, go through some of my other friend's houses to lose him, and then just run back to take his son out to play before he got back.

It was a challenge for me. I wouldn't tolerate someone judging me by my color. How come he let his son play with other black kids, but stopped him when it came to me?!

And so I went on coming back time and time again.

In the end he just gave up; I think he finally realized I was unstoppable and that I would go on playing with his son whether he liked it or not.

That memory still passes through my mind every now and then, and makes me wish that we were all more like children, and that we'd stop judging each other for all the stupid reasons we put between us. Why can't we all just accept each other for what we are and embrace our differences and accept them as enriching elements that make each one of us unique?

Moment of Silence

All: Jesus our friend and brother, through your life and your journey to the cross, your death and resurrection, you have shown us how to live in love. May we always follow your example, living in redemption, living a life of compassion, in the search for peace through justice for all your people.

(The following should be read by a Youth if one is present and willing.)

Ladies and Gentlemen - I'm only going to talk to you just for a minute or so this evening. Because...

I have some very sad news for all of you, and I think sad news for all of our fellow citizens, and people who love peace all over the world, and that is that Martin Luther King was shot and was killed tonight in Memphis, Tennessee.

Martin Luther King dedicated his life to love and to justice between fellow human beings. He died in the cause of that effort. In this difficult day, in this difficult time for the United States, it's perhaps well to ask what kind of a nation we are and what direction we want to move in.

For those of you who are black - considering the evidence evidently is that there were white people who were responsible - you can be filled with bitterness, and with hatred, and a desire for revenge.

We can move in that direction as a country, in greater polarization - black people amongst blacks, and white amongst whites, filled with hatred toward one another. Or we can make an effort, as Martin Luther King did, to understand and to comprehend, and replace that violence, that stain of bloodshed that has spread across our land, with an effort to understand, compassion and love.

For those of you who are black and are tempted to be filled with hatred and mistrust of the injustice of such an act, against all white people, I would only say that I can also feel in my own heart the same kind of feeling. I had a member of my family killed, but he was killed by a white man.

But we have to make an effort in the United States, we have to make an effort to understand, to get beyond these rather difficult times.

My favorite poet was Aeschylus. He once wrote: "Even in our sleep, pain which cannot forget falls drop by drop upon the heart, until, in our own despair, against our will, comes wisdom through the awful grace of God."

What we need in the United States is not division; what we need in the United States is not hatred; what we need in the United States is not violence and lawlessness, but is love and wisdom, and compassion toward one another, and a feeling of justice toward those who still suffer within our country, whether they be white or whether they be black.

(Interrupted by applause)

So I ask you tonight to return home, to say a prayer for the family of Martin Luther King, yeah that's true, but more importantly to say a prayer for our own country, which all of us love - a prayer for understanding and that compassion of which I spoke. We can do well in this country. We will have difficult times. We've had difficult times in the past. And we will have difficult times in the future. It is not the end of violence; it is not the end of lawlessness; and it's not the end of disorder.

But the vast majority of white people and the vast majority of black people in this country want to live together, want to improve the quality of our life, and want justice for all human beings that abide in our land.

(Interrupted by applause)

Let us dedicate ourselves to what the Greeks wrote so many years ago: to tame the savageness of man and make gentle the life of this world.

Let us dedicate ourselves to that, and say a prayer for our country and for our people. Thank you very much. (Applause)

Robert F. Kennedy - April 4, 1968

Just two months later, Robert Kennedy was gunned down during a celebration following his victory in the California primary, June 5, 1968.

Moment of Silence

"Darkness cannot drive out darkness,

only light can do that.

Hate cannot drive out hate;

only love can do that".

-Rev. Dr. Martin Luther King, Jr.

Leader:

Holy Trinity, we ask that you forgive us for the wrongs that we have done against each other. We thank you for bringing to this world such people as Rosa Parks, Rev. Dr. Martin Luther King, Jr. Caesar Chavez, Medgar Evers, Bobby Kennedy, Lyndon Johnson, Gandhi, Harriet Tubman, Sojourner Truth, Thurgood Marshal, Francisco Ramirez, Rev. Absalom Jones, John "Bud" Fowler, Paul Robeson, Rev. Richard Allen, Bp. James Theodore Holly, W.E.B. DuBois, Bp. Samuel David Ferguson, Rev. Pauli Murray, Jesse Owens, Eleanor Roosevelt and others who have worked and died for equality for all, and the saints no longer with us that we name now:

      (People are encouraged to say the names of other Saints that have **died** out loud)

and that we may follow in their example in Loving our neighbor as ourselves.

We thank you for those who have worked hard against Racism, Sexism, Homophobia, Classism, and for all of the other wrongs that we have done against each other. We also thank those who have taken the Anti-Racism training in this and other dioceses, and for those who give it.

Leader: Forgive us for remaining silent and bound by fear
All: Give us courage to speak and act with justice

Leader: Forgive us our arrogance in closing our eyes to other peoples and cultures
All: Forgive us for disfiguring this land and despoiling its bounty

Leader: Forgive us for despising the cultures of others, and taking away their self-respect
All: Give us grace to bind one another's wounds

Leader: Forgive us for not listening to the griefs of all who are oppressed in this land
All: Draw us together as one people

Leader: Forgive us for our prejudice and indifference towards those whose ways are different from our ways
All: Strengthen us to live with respect and compassion for one another

(All turn and fast each other in a circle if possible)

All:
I ask you my brothers and sisters in Christ, for forgiveness for the wrongs that I have done in the past towards you. From this time on, I will do my best to do no injustices towards all that I am with, and to be a shining example of the Love that the Holy Trinity has for us all.

Leader:
We are the body of Christ
All:
His spirit is with us

Leader:
May the Peace of the Lord be Always with you.
All:
And also with you.
(If this is being done in a church and/or a clergy person is present, Holy Communion can be held beginning here)

Leader:
Go in Peace to love and serve the Lord
All:
Thanks be to God.

Leader:
As you leave, please greet each other in the Peace.

Madonna & Child By Lorielle New

Stations Of The Cross

Alzheimer's: Do You Remember?

By Earl Clinton Williams, Jr.

<u>Acclamations</u>

I want to thank a very special person, who through her photography got me to think about putting this together. Her name is Nancy Duranteau. She had a photo exhibit that was shown at the Lakeview Branch of the Oakland Library, located in Oakland, Ca. Nancy is someone that makes me realize that there are great people in the world and I am glad that we have ended up involved in some way in different things within the Episcopal Diocese of California. The exhibit that she had contained photographs of a family member that suffered form the disease, and as I walked around looking at each picture on one trip to the library, I found myself making up a story about here life from birth until death, then I realized that in a way I was doing the Stations of The Cross. I then realized that there a huge number of stories that needed to be told so that others realized that they did not have to feel alone. I hope that this will help those that feel alone to know that they aren't alone, and will help those who are trying to get an understanding of what caregivers and others go through.

Station 1: Jesus in the Garden of Gethsemane

-

Leader: We adore you, oh Christ, and we bless you.
All: **Because by your holy cross you have redeemed the world.**

Reading:

Then Jesus came with them to a place called Gethsemane, and he said to his disciples, "Sit here while I go over there and pray." He took along Peter and the two sons of Zebedee, and began to feel sorrow and distress. Then he said to them, "My soul is sorrowful even to death. Remain here and keep watch with me." He advanced a little and fell prostrate in prayer, saying, "My Father, if it is possible, let this cup pass from me; yet, not as I will, but as you will." When he returned to his disciples he found them asleep. He said to Peter, "So you could not keep watch with me for one hour? Watch and pray that you may not undergo the test. The spirit is willing, but the flesh is weak."
Matthew 25:36-41

Moment of Silence

Story:

I had heard about the disease through stuff on television and on the news, but I never thought that I would have to be around someone with it. Boy was I wrong.

I had gotten a job with a company that did carpentry work in convalescent hospitals and nursing homes. We made the stuff that needed to put done at the business, then took our work to the place and installed it. I enjoyed the job when I began, as I started at the business and hadn't gone to do any installations. Then the time came to go out an install.

The first place that we had to install the stuff was located across the country and the person that I was working with and I flew there. We installed the stuff into most of the place, but there was still one area where we needed to do, but it was behind a set of doors that we had to get buzzed into. Some people on staff said that is where all of the Alzheimer patients were, and that we should be careful about where we put stuff as some of them would just steal things.

We went in and began our work. Things seemed pretty nice, and I figured that I would get through this with a breeze. It was going to take us about two days to get this area done, as we had started in the area pretty late in the day, so that meant we would have to come back into it the next day.

I was busy working along when I suddenly looked up to see a woman standing down the hall. Most of the time I would see patients and would keep on working, but this woman was beautiful. Just by her looks you would think that she was in her mid-forties, married with wonderful kids. I thought that she was either someone who worked there, or was a visitor. A few minutes went by, then one of the staff walked up to the woman and told her that she needed to go back into her room. I couldn't believe what I had just heard. The woman turned around and went into the room. As the staff member walked past me, I stopped her and asked if the woman was really a patient? The person told me that she was, and that the woman was in her 70s. I couldn't believe what I had just heard. It had to be a dream that I was having, for this really couldn't be true. I did some more work and my partner came over and said that we should be going as we had a long day ahead of us the next day. So I wasn't dreaming, that woman had to be a mirage, as I was tired.

We went back the next day and got back to work. Things were going smooth for me, then I look up to see two nurses walk down the hall and enter a room. I continued with my work then suddenly hear some banging. I look up to see one of the nurses coming out of the room, then I realized that it was the same room that I had saw the patient go into. Then I see a wheelchair come out. They wheel her by and she was as beautiful as I thought. I had a hard time continuing to work

We went to lunch, and I told my partner what happened, and he told me to not let it bother me. When we came back into the area, I did my best to not let it bother me, but I quickly learned to turn off of my emotions. From that point on, I learned how to turn my emotions on and off while working for that company when going into places, I had no choice.

I ask God to forgive me for what I had to do, and I am sure that God totally understands.

Moment of Silence

All: Jesus our friend and brother, through your life and your journey to the cross, your death and resurrection, you have shown us how to live in love. May we always follow your example, living in redemption, living a life of compassion, in the search for peace through justice for all your people.

Station 2: Jesus, Betrayed by Judas, is Arrested

Leader: We adore you, oh Christ, and we bless you.
All: **Because by your holy cross you have redeemed the world.**

Reading:

Then, while [Jesus] was still speaking, Judas, one of the Twelve, arrived, accompanied by a crowd with swords and clubs, who had come from the chief priests, the scribes, and the elders. His betrayer had arranged a signal with them, saying, "the man I shall kiss is the one; arrest him and lead him away securely." He came and immediately went over to him and said, "Rabbi." And he kissed him. At this they laid hands on him and arrested him.
Mark 14: 43-46

Moment of Silence

Story:

My Mother Is Slipping Away

By Dare2Love

Proud, active and independent
Always described my mother
Determined to live her life
Never depending on another

My mother was always particular about
Her looks, age, and appearance
Enjoying the love of several men
Sharing years of passion and romance

Her mental status is changing
Words come out jumbled and unclear
She forgets the names of loved ones
To forget me is something I fear

My heart is breaking
Trying to make her understand
The desire for independence
Now, an unreasonable demand

My Mother's eye sight is failing
Her world, now hard to see
It's difficult to comprehend
My mother's dependence on me

My tears come easily
As my mother slips away
I must enjoy each moment
Cherishing my mother each day

God please be merciful
When my mother's life is through
Send loved ones to greet her
Guiding her safely home to you

Moment of Silence

All: Jesus our friend and brother, through your life and your journey to the cross, your death and resurrection, you have shown us how to live in love. May we always follow your example, living in redemption, living a life of compassion, in the search for peace through justice for all your people.

Station 3: Jesus is Condemned by the Sanhedrin

Leader: We adore you, oh Christ, and we bless you.
All: **Because by your holy cross you have redeemed the world.**

Reading:

When day came the council of elders of the people met, both chief priests and scribes, and they brought him before their Sanhedrin. They said, "If you are the Messiah, tell us," but he replied to them, "If I tell you, you will not believe, and if I question, you will not respond. But from this time on the Son of Man will be seated at the right hand of the power of God." They all asked, "Are you then the Son of God?" He replied to them, "You say that I am." Then they said, "What further need have we for testimony? We have heard it from his own mouth."
Luke 22: 66-71

Moment of Silence

Story:

I miss my grandmother very much these days but the saddest thing is I miss her most when I am with her. I spent many days taking care of her but taking care of her physically seems easy compared to trying to care for her emotional needs. She is just so unhappy and mean. She wants her parents or husband and they have been gone for years. She wonders where my aunts and uncles are and thinks they are all still children. She seems to know I am someone that she knows but I am no longer her granddaughter. I am simply the young lady that constantly asks her questions and brings her cardinals. She is frightened most of the time that someone is going to steal something from her or hurt her in some way. Even when I get up well before daylight just for a few moments peace or I stay up late into the night, I can't escape her hurtful comments. She will awaken and demand to know who I am, why I am in her home, and why I am stealing from her. I try to sit next to her and tell her the many stories that I can remember from my childhood, quizzing her along the way to make sure she can remember theses things too. Of course she doesn't but she will say, "Oh yeah you are right. I remember that." I miss her most when I am with her.

The disease has been waging war on her brain for a long time, long before anyone even noticed it. It has made her mind an empty vessel. She looks up with nearly blank eyes that once twinkled with an overwhelming sweetness. Those eyes now search frantically for something - anything that feels like a real moment; anything that feels like a real memory. She searches her brain but unfortunately the disease has taken over her mind like barnacles on a sunken ship and will not release thoughts from the vessel easily. With its cold, calculated maneuvers, it has sought to deconstruct her completely, and I am sorry to say it has accomplished its goal. I miss her most when I am with her.

Once her beautiful spirit showed through her smile; however these days she rarely smiles and a grimace of confusion now is a constant. When she does manage a smile it is one of the saddest smiles one can imagine - the smile of frenzied desperation; desperation and fickle hope that this simple physical expression will manifest into reality, and she will have a moment of real happiness again. She is locked in her world of sorrow and no one has the key to release her. We can go there to her and visit but most days I become lost in her myself which is not healthy for me. What used to be beautiful creamy skin has been replaced by wrinkles and frown lines, drawn from a life of too much worry. The beautiful voice that once sang hymns in praise of her God now waivers with despair and the hands that once played glorious hymns are now withered and weak although she manages to play the piano for many hours each day, note by note, but only she recognizes the hymns she is playing in her mind. I miss her most when I am with her.

When I look into her eyes I see an abyss of desperation staring back at me. As she looks to me for answers, she seems less like my grams and more like a frightened child wanting the comfort of her mother's arms. I steel myself against the sadness at seeing her appear so small, for it is my turn to be her nurturer yet again today. Her confusion is punctuated by brief moments of lucidity. The secrets are housed deep within- where even she cannot always find them. When I hold her hand as she prepares for bed and I look deep into her eyes, there I see a spark of recognition in her eyes, far back in the recesses of her mutilated mind. Is it just my wishing that is making this happen or does she know who I am? After all I am of her, part of her, and we are blood relatives. How could she not recognize me after these many years? Yes I miss her most when I am with her

I was watching her sleep one night. I sat there and wondered if her dreams were filled with loss or if she is happy there. I wondered if her dreams were taking her to the places of the past where she openly longs to be in her waking hours. I decided to try to sleep because 4:00 am comes very early. I closed my eyes as I remember the many memories I have of this empty vessel. I can see her dancing the Charleston in her old living room as the music plays in the background. I can see her making mud pies in the yard with me and my cousins. I can see her teaching me about the many birds that came to our feeders walking along the garden paths. If only for a few moments, I am back in time with her and she is smiling and loving me. She is cheating at cards and laughing when she gets caught. Her hands are strong and she lifts me up to the water fountain. She turns me around assuredly and gives me a tight hug. Yes, I miss her most when I am with her.

Moment of Silence

All: Jesus our friend and brother, through your life and your journey to the cross, your death and resurrection, you have shown us how to live in love. May we always follow your example, living in redemption, living a life of compassion, in the search for peace through justice for all your people.

Station 4: Jesus is Denied by Peter

Leader: We adore you, oh Christ, and we bless you.
All: **Because by your holy cross you have redeemed the world.**

Reading:

Now Peter was sitting outside in the courtyard. One of the maids came over to him and said, "You too were with Jesus the Galilean." But he denied it in front of everyone, saying, "I do not know what you are talking about!" As he went out to the gate, another girl saw him and said to those who were there, "This man was with Jesus the Nazarene." Again he denied it with an oath, "I do not know the man!" A little later the bystanders came over and said to Peter, "Surely you too are one of them; even your speech gives you away." At that he began to curse and to swear, "I do not know the man." And immediately a cock crowed. Then Peter remembered the word that Jesus had spoken: "Before the cock crows you will deny me three times." He went out and began to weep bitterly.
Matthew 26: 69-75

Moment of Silence

Story:

My mother died of complications from Alzheimer's Disease. It was a horrible thing to witness, and I can only guess at the terror one must feel at the realization that this disease has taken hold. Alzheimer's patients have a recognizably vacant stare; two of my friends who've also lost someone to it agree that the patient gets that 'look' that says, what am I doing here? and who are you?

When my mother was in palliative care for the last two weeks of her battle with Alzheimer's, her body had become so atrophied by lack of movement that her pain was excruciating every time they changed her position. We begged the nurses to give her more of 'something' for the pain. I wonder if it was our mother's comfort we were seeking, or our own. There is no more helpless feeling in the world than watching someone die of memory loss, as the Alzheimer's patient gradually forgets everything they've ever learned, but in reverse order, so that the very last thing they forget is how to breathe.

Considering that my mother's sister also died from it, there's a good chance that a couple of my siblings and I might inherit the gene. If I begin to realize that my mind is being stolen moment by moment, that's when I plan to take a long walk in some dark, winter woods.

Moment of Silence

All: Jesus our friend and brother, through your life and your journey to the cross, your death and resurrection, you have shown us how to live in love. May we always follow your example, living in redemption, living a life of compassion, in the search for peace through justice for all your people.

Station 5: Jesus is Judged by Pilate

Leader: We adore you, oh Christ, and we bless you.
All: **Because by your holy cross you have redeemed the world.**

Reading:

The chief priests with the elders and the scribes, that is, the whole Sanhedrin, held a council. They bound Jesus, led him away, and handed him over to Pilate. Pilate questioned him, "Are you the king of the Jews?" He said to him in reply, "You say so." The chief priests accused him of many things. Again Pilate questioned him, "Have you no answer? See how many things they accuse you of." Jesus gave him no further answer, so that Pilate was amazed.... Pilate, wishing to satisfy the crowd, released Barrabas... [and] handed [Jesus] over to be crucified.
Mark 15: 1-5, 15

Moment of Silence

Story:

Dad died Oct 6th, 2005. The year of the Veteran, and he was one of Canada's youngest. He had lied about his age, and was only 17 when he went overseas to fight in WW2.

His army records note him as a "Bright, keen, young man, slight in built with an above average learning ability" He later performed in the Canadian Army Shows. He was a avid golfer, a competitive hockey player, a championship curling player and an avid golfer who attained TWO (yes 2) Holes in Ones. (not too surprising He was a Twin& had twins himself). He held his own golf tournaments and complied an impressive collection of jazz music. The great (Satch imo) himself personally remembers him fondly in the Louis Armstrong Museum.

During the last few years of his life he no longer knew me. Those were difficult years for me, but it was not about me, it was about him.

One conversation we had when he had been told about his Alzheimer's still stands in my mind. "They say that I will not know you, but I don't believe that. There will always be something inside me that will know you". Well just two years later because I had been exposed to SAR's I could not visit him for six weeks, that was all it took, for me to be erased from his memory. After that I was just a nice lady who came to visit with him.

However, he kept his promise, just as he was entering into the last stages of this despicable disease and the dieing process, had begun, we had taken him to a family reunion. As we were trying to get him into the car, he he had not been talking for quite some time, so you can imagine my surprise when he stood tall called out my name, and said. "You are here! I knew you would always be here for me".

Two weeks later he was in the hospital. During that last month, he was talking to us, knew us and knew his family. It was a miracle. I believe that as his body was dieing to the flesh, his spirit was so strong that it superseded the physical realm. What a blessing! but then he had always kept his word to me. Still cry, still miss him, but I know that one day I will meet him in the clouds. What a party that will be. The written word confirms it, I believe it that settles it. Love you Dad

Moment of Silence

All: Jesus our friend and brother, through your life and your journey to the cross, your death and resurrection, you have shown us how to live in love. May we always follow your example, living in redemption, living a life of compassion, in the search for peace through justice for all your people.

Station 6: Jesus is Scourged and Crowned with Thorns

Leader: We adore you, oh Christ, and we bless you.
All: **Because by your holy cross you have redeemed the world.**

Reading:

Then Pilate took Jesus and had him scourged. And the soldiers wove a crown out of thorns and placed it on his head, and clothed him in a purple cloak, and they came to him and said,"Hail, King of the Jews!" And they struck him repeatedly.
John 19: 1-3

Moment of Silence

Story:

My grandmother had Alzheimers.

It became official when I was six years old. My grandfather had been hiding it for a long time, no-one can be sure of how long, but he had been dressing her, correcting her conversation which was never that much as she was a very quiet woman and generally keeping her at home and to herself as he was afraid to loose her to a nursing home.

Then one day, my parents and I went to visit and found her crying on the windowsill, very scared that an old strange man was inside the house and that was my grandfather.

She was then wrongly put into a very severe mental hospital and whilst she was here the neighboring patient tried to set her bed on fire whilst she was asleep. My grandmother was there for three days and then taken into a Nursing Home, she never recognized anyone from then until one day before her death.

She forgot how to eat, she recognized no-one and lost all speech patterns and shrunk to four stone. Two things that were a habitual habit were buying her ice-cream and spoon feeding her this and also reading her Psalm 23 as these were two of her favorite things.

She died when I was aged 11, the day before her death she firstly said 'Good morning' and asked the nursing assistant how she was. She then when I visited with my mum and dad, spoke to me by name and asked how i was and thanked me for visiting her every week, she then also spoke very shortly, a sentence to each of the family to verify she knew us all and then died that night.

I think of it as her death being akin to the legend of the mute swan - they live their life in silence and then just before their death they summon forth a loud call.

Moment of Silence

All: Jesus our friend and brother, through your life and your journey to the cross, your death and resurrection, you have shown us how to live in love. May we always follow your example, living in redemption, living a life of compassion, in the search for peace through justice for all your people.

Station 7: Jesus Bears the Cross

Leader: We adore you, oh Christ, and we bless you.
All: **Because by your holy cross you have redeemed the world.**

Reading:

When the chief priests and the guards saw [Jesus] they cried out, "Crucify him, crucify him!" Pilate said to them, "Take him yourselves and crucify him. I find no guilt in him." ... They cried out, "Take him away, take him away! Crucify him!" Pilate said to them, "Shall I crucify your king?" The chief priests answered, "We have no king but Caesar." Then he handed him over to them to be crucified. So they took Jesus, and carrying the cross himself he went out to what is called the Place of the Skull, in Hebrew, Golgotha. John 19: 6, 15-17

Moment of Silence

Story:

My Dad started getting dementia several years ago. A relative lived with him and took advantage of him. I tried to get him committed, so that the stealing and abuse would stop. Everyone said I was doing the right thing. Except the doctor, finally, who released him back to his home. For three years I couldn't go to his house. I slowly became friends with him again, he basically doesn't remember anything. It finally got to the point he didn't want to spend the night at his house because of the person living there. I took him in for several weeks and now he is safe at a nursing facility with round the clock care. His house is in shambles. His taxes and his finances are in shambles because the relative took advantage in every possible way. His family is a shambles as we all live in defense of criticism for our dysfunction. At least now I am doing something for my Dad, but he doesn't really know whats going on. Nursing homes are not perfect, but his house is a condemned wreck. When he lived with me I was up all hours of the night and it put an incredible strain on my 30 year marriage. Now Medicaid is going to get whatever is left as I work to keep his funds drawing down to pay for his care. I'm not angry at my Dad like I used to be, because really without a lawyer to tell you what to do, you're as good as screwed in our country when it comes to your inheritance. Unless you manage to die at a decent young age. All of this has left me morbid and scheming in my mind how I can avoid being a burden to my own children in a few years. I'm ready to give them control of my money right now, if I could. I've found myself wishing euthanasia was accepted by our society so I could go gracefully before I lose my mind.

Moment of Silence

All: Jesus our friend and brother, through your life and your journey to the cross, your death and resurrection, you have shown us how to live in love. May we always follow your example, living in redemption, living a life of compassion, in the search for peace through justice for all your people.

Station 8: Jesus is Helped by Simon the Cyrenian to Carry the Cross

Leader: We adore you, oh Christ, and we bless you.
All: **Because by your holy cross you have redeemed the world.**

Reading:

They pressed into service a passer-by, Simon, a Cyrenian, who was coming in from the country, the father of Alexander and Rufus, to carry his cross.
Mark 15: 21

Moment of Silence

Story:

My mother died of Alzheimer's on August 30th of this year. She died in my house surrounded by love and sadness by her family.

I needed a moment after she passed and stepped out onto the patio. It was a cool day for August and I was surprised at how fast she left in the end and how I couldn't feel her spirit at all anymore. It was like she had passed through the eye of the needle in a quicksilver second and had gone on to where she needed to be as fast as it takes the heart to beat just once. I looked up to the sky and suddenly one little section of the sky rained down, like God was shedding his tears for her. The leaves on the tree were waving in a crisp breeze as if to send her on her way. It all lasted for a few moments and when it was done, the crickets came out and started to chirp.

As I paused at the door, my little 3 year old niece said "The crickets are here and they are saying good-bye to Oma too" and she was exactly right. Me, my niece, nature and God all came together to say good-bye and the moment moved on to one of love and peace. God speed mom.

Moment of Silence

All: Jesus our friend and brother, through your life and your journey to the cross, your death and resurrection, you have shown us how to live in love. May we always follow your example, living in redemption, living a life of compassion, in the search for peace through justice for all your people.

Station 9: Jesus Meets the Women of Jerusalem

Leader: We adore you, oh Christ, and we bless you.
All: **Because by your holy cross you have redeemed the world.**

Reading:

A large crowd of people followed Jesus, including many women who mourned and lamented him. Jesus turned to them and said, "Daughters of Jerusalem, do not weep for me; weep instead for yourselves and for your children, for indeed, the days are coming when people will say, 'Blessed are the barren, the wombs that never bore and the breasts that never nursed.' At that time, people will say to the mountains, 'Fall upon us!' and to the hills, 'Cover us!' for if these things are done when the wood is green what will happen when it is dry?"
Luke 23: 27-31

Moment of Silence

Story:

My mother has been in a nursing home, with Alzheimer's, for eight years now. She herself made the decision to go, for which I am very grateful to have been spared. She is 88 now, and I am 61, and my husband is in his 70's. Here we are, seniors looking after seniors. Many of our friends are also looking after aged, helpless parents who who not remember them, and who require special, constant care. Mum was always a gentle, sweet-natured woman, protective, loving and proud of us. She does not know us now, which is the most difficult thing to deal with. The woman who was my mother is really gone, and I have grieved for her. Mum has never become violent or fearful, as many Alzheimer's patients do. She believes she is the doctor in her nursing home, and she visits her patients every day (all her fellow residents). Although she doesn't remember who anyone is, she is very happy and always sweet and cheerful. I am grateful for that, too. We live thousands of miles from her, and it is sometimes really difficult to handle all her affairs and needs from so far away, but she looked after me when I was a helpless child, and now I look after her. I just wish she knew me. I phone her from time to time. She is very glad to get a call, but has no idea who she is talking to. I know not to take it personally, but it still hurts a little.

I do worry about my own future. My mother is one of four sisters, two of whom got Alzheimer's. Mum's mum had it, and so did my maternal great grandmother. I hope I am one of the lucky ones who escape the disease, but just in case, I have given my husband and children instructions on what to do if I do fall victim, and made my arrangements ahead of time.

May I end with a story I think is very funny? This was years ago, when my Alzheimer's grandmother was living with our family. Mum and I were sitting in the kitchen when my grandmother came in, and demanded for the thousandth time, in her impeccable British accent, "Where is my husband?" Patiently my mother answered, "Now, Mother, you know Dad died two years ago." "Oh", said Grandma, greatly surprised, then, curiously, "Well, who died first - him or me?"

Moment of Silence

All: Jesus our friend and brother, through your life and your journey to the cross, your death and resurrection, you have shown us how to live in love. May we always follow your example, living in redemption, living a life of compassion, in the search for peace through justice for all your people.

Station 10: Jesus is Crucified

Leader: We adore you, oh Christ, and we bless you.
All: **Because by your holy cross you have redeemed the world.**

Reading:

When they came to the place called the Skull, they crucified him and the criminals there, one on his right, the other on his left. [Then Jesus said, "Father, forgive them, they know not what they do."] *Luke 23: 33-34*

Moment of Silence

10 Tips for Living with Early Onset Alzheimer's
1. Expect to have good days and bad days.
2. Share your story — educate others and express yourself.
3. Discuss changes in relationships with a counselor.
4. Talk openly about the changes the disease is causing. Share feelings with friends and family, and someone who can help with spiritual needs.
5. Get involved. Volunteer in your community. Become an advocate.
6. Talk to your employer about adapting your job hours or duties.
7. Get professional legal and financial help.
8. Maintain your health and reduce stress.
9. Take steps to make your home a safer place.
10. Stay active. Keep making memories with your loved ones. Use your experience to enlighten.

Moment of Silence

All: Jesus our friend and brother, through your life and your journey to the cross, your death and resurrection, you have shown us how to live in love. May we always follow your example, living in redemption, living a life of compassion, in the search for peace through justice for all your people.

Station 11: Jesus Promises His Kingdom to the Good Thief

Leader: We adore you, oh Christ, and we bless you.
All: **Because by your holy cross you have redeemed the world.**

Reading:

Now one of the criminals hanging there reviled Jesus, saying, "Are you not the Messiah? Save yourself and us." The other, however, rebuking him, said in reply, "Have you no fear of God, for you are subject to the same condemnation? And indeed, we have been condemned justly, for the sentence we received corresponds to our crimes, but this man has done nothing criminal." Then he said, "Jesus, remember me when you come into your kingdom." He replied to him, "Amen, I say to you, today you will be with me in Paradise."
Luke 23: 39-43

Moment of Silence

Sharing your diagnosis

Talking about your diagnosis is important for helping people understand Alzheimer's disease and learning about how they can continue to be a part of your life. The following suggestions may help:

> ⌃Explain that Alzheimer's disease is not a normal part of aging but a disease of the brain that results in impaired memory, thinking and behavior.

> ⌃Share educational information on Alzheimer's disease or invite family and friends to attend Alzheimer's education programs.

> ⌃Be honest about how you feel about your diagnosis and allow other family members to do the same.

> ⌃Assure friends that although the disease will change your life, you want to continue enjoying their company.

> ⌃Let family and friends know when and how you may need their help and support.

Moment of Silence

All: Jesus our friend and brother, through your life and your journey to the cross, your death and resurrection, you have shown us how to live in love. May we always follow your example, living in redemption, living a life of compassion, in the search for peace through justice for all your people.

Station 12: Jesus Speaks to His Mother and the Disciple

Leader: We adore you, oh Christ, and we bless you.
All: **Because by your holy cross you have redeemed the world.**

Reading:

Standing by the cross of Jesus were his mother and his mother's sister, Mary the wife of Clopas, and Mary of Magdala. When Jesus saw his mother and the disciple there whom he loved, he said to his mother, "Woman, behold, your son." Then he said to the disciple, "Behold, your mother." And from that hour the disciple took her into his home.
John 19: 25-27

Moment of Silence

Working with your partner

Most people with Alzheimer's disease continue to live at home even as the disease progresses. As a result, your partner may have to manage the household and your care. He or she may feel a sense of loss because of the changes the disease brings to your relationship. The following suggestions may benefit your relationship:

⚓ Continue to participate in as many activities as you can.

⚓ Modify activities to your changing abilities.

⚓ Talk with your partner about how he or she can assist you.

⚓ Work together to gather information about caregiver services and their costs, such as housekeeping and respite care, and start a file you can consult when they are needed.

⚓ Seek professional counseling to discuss new factors in your relationship and changes in sexual relations.

⚓ Continue to find ways in which you and your partner can fulfill the need for intimacy.

⚓ Encourage your partner to attend a support group for caregivers.

Moment of Silence

All: Jesus our friend and brother, through your life and your journey to the cross, your death and resurrection, you have shown us how to live in love. May we always follow your example, living in redemption, living a life of compassion, in the search for peace through justice for all your people.

Station 13: Jesus Dies on the Cross

Leader: We adore you, oh Christ, and we bless you.
All: **Because by your holy cross you have redeemed the world.**

Reading:

It was now about noon and darkness came over the whole land until three in the afternoon because of an eclipse of the sun. Then the veil of the temple was torn down the middle. Jesus cried out in a loud voice, "Father, into your hands I commend my spirit"; and when he had said this he breathed his last. *Luke 23: 44-46*

Moment of Silence

Story:

My brother & I decided NOT to tell our late mom that she had Alzheimer's. She'd been perfectly fine mentally , altho under severe stress while caring for our dad who had terminal cancer. After he died..she woke up & found him one morning...she went into a depression & then developed memory problems. She took dad's death personally & it brought back the memories of every relative she ever had that died. She felt that she was being punished somehow & that fate was against her.
We did a lot of praying together & that helped her to feel better about accepting dad's loss as well as the others'. We had her treated for depression & it went away but the memory problems persisted & got worse. We had her tested & she was diagnosed with AD. Her brother also got it after a skull fracture in an accident but since he lived out of state & she rarely saw him, we didn't tell her about him after we found out about it.
Mom knew something was wrong with her memory & was scared she might be losing her mind. We had gut feelings that if we told her she had such a HORRIBLE disease it would destroy her because it would bring back those feelings of punishment & fate being against her plus the feelings of the loss of other relatives all magnified by the new fact that now she'd been picked to lose her very MIND. We decided to tell her she still had depression from grief over dad. She was able to handle that quite well.
I put her in a drug trial for Cognex which gave her another 1 1/2 good years in which I was able to take her to movies, concerts,visits to old pals , & relatives & in general pay her back for all she'd done for me over the years before she got to the point when she had to go into a nursing home.
I'm sure that I wouldn't have been able to give her those last good times if she'd known all along about the AD.

Moment of Silence

All: Jesus our friend and brother, through your life and your journey to the cross, your death and resurrection, you have shown us how to live in love. May we always follow your example, living in redemption, living a life of compassion, in the search for peace through justice for all your people.

Station 14: Jesus is Placed in the Tomb

Leader: We adore you, oh Christ, and we bless you.
All: **Because by your holy cross you have redeemed the world.**

Reading:

When it was evening, there came a rich man from Arimathea named Joseph, who was himself a disciple of Jesus. He went to Pilate and asked for the body of Jesus; then Pilate ordered it to be handed over. Taking the body, Joseph wrapped it [in] clean linen and laid it in his new tomb that he had hewn in the rock. Then he rolled a huge stone across the entrance to the tomb and departed. *Matthew 27: 57-60*

Moment of Silence

Story:

I would like to first start by saying that Alzheimer's has changed my life a lot for the better.

I am 21-years-old and I work in a nursing facility. Every day to me is a new tale, even though I do the same thing. I am responsible for the care of Alzheimer's patients, many with end-stage dementia. My shift starts at 7:00 am, I go into report and get started with my day.

My first patient, I wash him up, put him on a lift and get him started for the day. While with this patient I am often groped, hollered at and even hit. Many of the patients I care for are very combative.

After my first patient, its down the hall to the next, she is a lovely woman, in her 70s, loves to dance and rock in her wheelchair to Elvis or any other upbeat music on in our dining room. She is one of the people I have made breakthroughs with. I like to keep her on her feet and walking as much as possible -- after all, in life it is important to use what you have so you don't lose it. This is one thing I live by while I am at work, I like to keep my patients as active as possible even though most can't do that much.

Breakfast starts at 9:00 am so I don't have much time to get the rest of my patients up out of bed, which I always try to do. Now I go and see another lady. Every morning we get up and walk to the bathroom, get cleaned up and dressed for breakfast. I can say that this woman has a smile to die for, there's not much that gets her spirits down, that really makes me feel confident that I am doing my job well.

Though I remember one day in the dining room we were [giving] breakfast and one patient was feeding herself some bread. I came up and noticed that she was rocking back and forth quickly and then saw her lips turning blue. To me it was obvious that she was choking. I got behind her chair and began the Heimlich. I thank God within seconds the piece of bread lodged in her throat flew out and she caught her breath and was OK.

It's moments like that really make you realize how delicate life is. I love my job, and all of the wonderful people I get to care for each day. Everyone tells me what a good person I am for being able to do what I do so well, and they are right, but I couldn't do it if I didn't have the heart that I do. With this heart I would do anything for my patients to make their quality of life better when they are at their worst.

Moment of Silence

All: Jesus our friend and brother, through your life and your journey to the cross, your death and resurrection, you have shown us how to live in love. May we always follow your example, living in redemption, living a life of compassion, in the search for peace through justice for all your people.

Pope by Lorielle New

Stations Of The Cross

Make Me Think

By Earl Clinton Williams, Jr.

Acclamations

What you are about to read and experience will hopefully make you think about the things that you do and how you can help to not only help the world to become a place where this subject will become a thing of the past, but it will hopefully help you into making better choices in the way that you treat others.

I would like to thank my parents, sister, nephews, aunts, uncles, cousins, the Quakers, The Episcopal Church, and those of other faiths who helped me to become the person that I am.

I would also like to give thanks to the Holy Trinity in guiding me through the process of putting this together. I only hope and pray that this is an instrument that will help this world become a better place.

I hope and pray that all of those that read and hear the stories to come will do an Act of Kindness to others, and when it is done to them that they Pass It Forward. Always remember YCMAD (You Can Make A Difference)

I would like to thank Lorielle New, an actress, artist and friend who made the picture that is on the front of these Stations. The title of the piece is Africa and is from her Icon Series. St. Jame's Episcopal Church in Oakland, Ca. has a copy of this piece hanging in it's chapel. If you would be interested in seeing more of her wonderful work, and would be interested in buying a copy of her artwork, please visit www.loriellenew.com as she has it for sale. She has full copyright to the artwork, and it has been used here with her permission.

Station 1: Jesus in the Garden of Gethsemane

Leader: We adore you, oh Christ, and we bless you.
All: **Because by your holy cross you have redeemed the world.**

Reading:

Then Jesus came with them to a place called Gethsemane, and he said to his disciples, "Sit here while I go over there and pray." He took along Peter and the two sons of Zebedee, and began to feel sorrow and distress. Then he said to them, "My soul is sorrowful even to death. Remain here and keep watch with me." He advanced a little and fell prostrate in prayer, saying, "My Father, if it is possible, let this cup pass from me; yet, not as I will, but as you will." When he returned to his disciples he found them asleep. He said to Peter, "So you could not keep watch with me for one hour? Watch and pray that you may not undergo the test. The spirit is willing, but the flesh is weak."
Matthew 25:36-41

Moment of Silence

Leader: In the name of the Father

Today, my brother is a lead software engineer with a major Internet website. While he was home visiting our rural hometown last week the local news interviewed him. "What's the #1 thing that contributed to your success in software engineering?" the reporter asked. "Well, I had two loves when I was a kid," my brother said. "One was basketball and the other was computer programming. When I lost my legs in a car accident at age 16 I was devastated. Basketball was no longer an option. So I poured my heart into programming and ended up falling in love with it over and over again. Which is foundation of why I'm sitting here with you now."

Moment of Silence

Leader: In the name of the Son

Today, the kid who bullied me in high school for four years straight is one week shy of being evicted from his apartment after being unemployed for the last six months. He showed up at my office this morning practically begging for work and forgiveness. After an hour of reflection, I've decided to give him both. I hope I made the right decision.

Moment of Silence

Leader: In the name of the Holy Spirit

Today, my little brother's internet start-up was purchased for $12,000,000. My brother is 17 years younger than me. Our parent's passed away in a car accident while I was babysitting him 17 years ago. I was 18 at the time and he was one. I took legal guardianship of him and worked two jobs for 16 years to make sure he had every opportunity in the world. He started his company at 18 just after he graduated high school. It took off like wildfire. This evening, he transferred $1,000,000 into my retirement savings account.

All: Jesus our friend and brother, through your life and your journey to the cross, your death and resurrection, you have shown us how to live in love. May we always follow your example, living in redemption, living a life of compassion, in the search for peace through justice for all your people.

Station 2: Jesus, Betrayed by Judas, is Arrested

Leader: We adore you, oh Christ, and we bless you.
All: **Because by your holy cross you have redeemed the world.**

Reading:

Then, while [Jesus] was still speaking, Judas, one of the Twelve, arrived, accompanied by a crowd with swords and clubs, who had come from the chief priests, the scribes, and the elders. His betrayer had arranged a signal with them, saying, "the man I shall kiss is the one; arrest him and lead him away securely." He came and immediately went over to him and said, "Rabbi." And he kissed him. At this they laid hands on him and arrested him.
Mark 14: 43-46

Moment of Silence

Leader: In the name of the Father

Today in Santo Domingo, roughly ten seconds after I gave a street peddler some change, a man walked out of an alleyway with a knife and tried to mug me. The street peddler walked up behind the mugger and slammed a broomstick across the side of his head, knocking him out cold.

Moment of Silence

Leader: In the name of the Son

Today, a young teenage boy was in line in front of me at Target. He used a gift card to buy two video games. The cashier, an older woman probably in her late 60's, rang him up and informed him that he had $12 remaining on his gift card. "Oh, wait then," he said as he ran two isles over and grabbed a $10 bouquet of flowers. As the cashier added the flowers to his order the boy handed them to her and said, "These are for you." The cashier could not wipe the smile off her face, even after he left.

Moment of Silence

Leader: In the name of the Holy Spirit

Today, my father said, "You've got to forgive him and move on." "He doesn't deserve to be forgiven!" I cried. "Don't do it for him," my father said. "Do it for yourself."

All: Jesus our friend and brother, through your life and your journey to the cross, your death and resurrection, you have shown us how to live in love. May we always follow your example, living in redemption, living a life of compassion, in the search for peace through justice for all your people.

Station 3: Jesus is Condemned by the Sanhedrin

Leader: We adore you, oh Christ, and we bless you.
All: **Because by your holy cross you have redeemed the world.**

Reading:

When day came the council of elders of the people met, both chief priests and scribes, and they brought him before their Sanhedrin. They said, "If you are the Messiah, tell us," but he replied to them, "If I tell you, you will not believe, and if I question, you will not respond. But from this time on the Son of Man will be seated at the right hand of the power of God." They all asked, "Are you then the Son of God?" He replied to them, "You say that I am." Then they said, "What further need have we for testimony? We have heard it from his own mouth."
Luke 22: 66-71

Moment of Silence

Leader: In the name of the Father
Today, it's been almost four months since my son's seven-year-old dog, Grover, got lost at a crowded fair on the outskirts of Orlando, Florida. We were on a family vacation visiting my husband's parents. We searched for him everywhere, put up fliers all over the city - the whole nine yards. Nothing. My son was devastated. This afternoon, Grover showed up at our front door in Austin, Texas all by himself.

Moment of Silence

Leader: In the name of the Son
Today, I am dying of Leukemia at age 16. I was sent home from the hospital for my final few weeks 152 days ago. But I am back at the hospital being treated again, because my doctors now believe there is hope.

Moment Of Silence

Leader: In the name of the Holy Spirit
Today, my son showed up to the diner for our weekly lunch date a few minutes late without a baseball cap on. "I can't even remember the last time you showed up without a cap," I said. "Actually, it's kind of a funny story," he said. "I've never told you about him, but every week on my walk here a homeless man who hangs out in the park down the street compliments my hat. So today, I stopped and talked to him for a few minutes. I found out that his name is Kyle, and I decided to give Kyle my hat. He was so happy. And next week when I walk by we'll have matching hats."

All: Jesus our friend and brother, through your life and your journey to the cross, your death and resurrection, you have shown us how to live in love. May we always follow your example, living in redemption, living a life of compassion, in the search for peace through justice for all your people.

Station 4: Jesus is Denied by Peter

Leader: We adore you, oh Christ, and we bless you.
All: **Because by your holy cross you have redeemed the world.**

Reading:

Now Peter was sitting outside in the courtyard. One of the maids came over to him and said, "You too were with Jesus the Galilean." But he denied it in front of everyone, saying, "I do not know what you are talking about!" As he went out to the gate, another girl saw him and said to those who were there, "This man was with Jesus the Nazorean." Again he denied it with an oath, "I do not know the man!" A little later the bystanders came over and said to Peter, "Surely you too are one of them; even your speech gives you away." At that he began to curse and to swear, "I do not know the man." And immediately a cock crowed. Then Peter remembered the word that Jesus had spoken: "Before the cock crows you will deny me three times." He went out and began to weep bitterly.
Matthew 26: 69-75

Moment of Silence

Leader: In the name of the Father
Today, my landscaping business partner and I were laying fresh sod in front of a new house. As we were working I was complaining about my relationship with my wife – how things haven't been quite as magical as they once were. "When was the last time you cooked dinner for her, or took her out on a romantic date?" my partner asked. "It's been awhile," I said. "Well, the grass is always greener in the areas where you water it," he replied.

Moment of Silence

Leader: In the name of the Son
Today, I was sitting on a park bench on the verge of tears like I have been for the last five days since my mom passed away. A little girl ran up to me smiling and said, "You look sad, so I picked these for you. I hope you feel better." Then she handed me a few dozen wildflowers wrapped into a bouquet with a little vine and gave me a big hug. And I smiled for the first time in five days.

Moment of Silence

Leader: In the name of the Holy Spirit
Today, I sat with her for two straight hours. She cried and let it all out. I listened. I nodded. I hugged her. And for awhile we simply sat in silence together. But I never said a word. This evening, just after dinner, she showed up at my front door again. "Thank you," she said. "I don't even remember what you told me earlier, but I feel like you gave me the best advice ever."

All: Jesus our friend and brother, through your life and your journey to the cross, your death and resurrection, you have shown us how to live in love. May we always follow your example, living in redemption, living a life of compassion, in the search for peace through justice for all your people.

Station 5: Jesus is Judged by Pilate

Leader: We adore you, oh Christ, and we bless you.
All: **Because by your holy cross you have redeemed the world.**

Reading:

 The chief priests with the elders and the scribes, that is, the whole Sanhedrin, held a council. They bound Jesus, led him away, and handed him over to Pilate. Pilate questioned him, "Are you the king of the Jews?" He said to him in reply, "You say so." The chief priests accused him of many things. Again Pilate questioned him, "Have you no answer? See how many things they accuse you of." Jesus gave him no further answer, so that Pilate was amazed.... Pilate, wishing to satisfy the crowd, released Barrabas... [and] handed [Jesus] over to be crucified.
Mark 15: 1-5, 15

Moment of Silence

Leader: In the name of the Father
 Today, as we were slowing down at a red light, my father scolded me for not having my seat belt on. No more than a second after the clicking sound of me buckling my seat belt, our small car was clipped from behind by a pick-up truck, spinning us 180 degrees in the middle of the street. Because we both had our seat belts on, and the fact that the impact came from behind, my father and I walked away with minor injuries.

Moment of Silence

Leader: In the name of the Son
 Today, at 4PM I pulled over to help a man (who turned out to be a paramedic) push his car out of the road. After looking under the hood for a few minutes we both agreed his radiator needed to be replaced. He told me he was running late to work, so I used my AAA card to get him a free tow and ride to a repair shop next to the hospital. Exactly an hour later I called 911 when my son's best friend fainted and stopped breathing after an asthma attack. The same paramedic, Jake, showed up at my house, performed CPR on my son's friend until he was breathing again, and took him to the hospital.

Moment of Silence

Leader: In the name of the Holy Spirit
 Today, my husband is a nurse at a children's psychiatric hospital. He comes home fairly often with bruises, torn clothes, and stains on his shirt from altercations with his patients. But it doesn't bother him at all. In fact, he usually tells me stories about his day with a smile across his face. He absolutely loves helping these children. My husband's giant heart.

All: Jesus our friend and brother, through your life and your journey to the cross, your death and resurrection, you have shown us how to live in love. May we always follow your example, living in redemption, living a life of compassion, in the search for peace through justice for all your people.

Station 6: Jesus is Scourged and Crowned with Thorns

Leader: We adore you, oh Christ, and we bless you.
All: **Because by your holy cross you have redeemed the world.**

Reading:

Then Pilate took Jesus and had him scourged. And the soldiers wove a crown out of thorns and placed it on his head, and clothed him in a purple cloak, and they came to him and said,"Hail, King of the Jews!" And they struck him repeatedly.

John 19: 1-3

Moment of Silence

Leader: In the name of the Father
Today, 9 years after their divorce, my dad and mom are back to living under the same roof. My mom's house washed away in the recent flood in North Dakota. My dad and step-mom's house fared better on higher ground. So they invited my mom to move in until she can salvage what's left of her house and rebuild.

Moment of Silence

Leader: In the name of the Son
Today, four days before my 8-year-old son and I would be evicted from our apartment, a family owned hotel and resort hired me and gave me an unexpected $3500 signing bonus – the exact amount I needed to avoid eviction. The owner delivered the bonus to me personally. She said, "All the people I talked to during your background check had great things to say about you, except your landlord. I know what it feels like to be out of work. I was once in your shoes. Welcome aboard."

Moment of Silence

Leader: In the name of the Holy Spirit
Today, due to Alzheimer's and dementia, my grandfather usually can't remember who my grandmother is when he wakes up in the morning. It bothered my grandmother a year ago when it first happened, but now she's fully supportive of his condition. In fact, she plays a game every day in which she tries to get my grandfather to ask her to re-marry him before dinnertime. She hasn't failed yet.

All: Jesus our friend and brother, through your life and your journey to the cross, your death and resurrection, you have shown us how to live in love. May we always follow your example, living in redemption, living a life of compassion, in the search for peace through justice for all your people.

Station 7: Jesus Bears the Cross

Leader: We adore you, oh Christ, and we bless you.

All: **Because by your holy cross you have redeemed the world.**

Reading:

When the chief priests and the guards saw [Jesus] they cried out, "Crucify him, crucify him!" Pilate said to them, "Take him yourselves and crucify him. I find no guilt in him." ... They cried out, "Take him away, take him away! Crucify him!" Pilate said to them, "Shall I crucify your king?" The chief priests answered, "We have no king but Caesar." Then he handed him over to them to be crucified. So they took Jesus, and carrying the cross himself he went out to what is called the Place of the Skull, in Hebrew, Golgotha. John 19: 6, 15-17

Moment of Silence

Leader: In the name of the Father
Today, I walked my daughter down the aisle. Ten years ago I pulled a 14 year old boy out of his mom's fire-engulfed SUV after a serious accident. Doctors initially said he would never walk again. My daughter came with me several times to visit him at the hospital. Then she started going on her own. Today, seeing him defy the odds and smile widely, standing on his own two feet at the altar as he placed a ring on my daughter's finger.

Moment of Silence

Leader: In the name of the Son
Today, my grandfather used 25 different coupons at the grocery store. Then he gave the money he saved to the bag boy as a tip. He does this almost every Sunday because he says he "likes to see people smile."

Moment of Silence

Leader: In the name of the Holy Spirit
Today, I have been a firefighter for 24 years. Back in 1992, the local newspapers and news channels called me a hero and interviewed me a few times after I carried 19 retirees, one at a time, out of a burning luxury retirement condo. I was off-duty at the time and just happened to be visiting my grandmother who lived across the street. This evening I was contacted by a trust attorney representing one of the retirees who I helped that day. She passed away yesterday, and in her will she left me 25% of her estate - roughly $800,000.

All: Jesus our friend and brother, through your life and your journey to the cross, your death and resurrection, you have shown us how to live in love. May we always follow your example, living in redemption, living a life of compassion, in the search for peace through justice for all your people.

Station 8: Jesus is Helped by Simon the Cyrenian to Carry the Cross

Leader: We adore you, oh Christ, and we bless you.
All: **Because by your holy cross you have redeemed the world.**

Reading:

They pressed into service a passer-by, Simon, a Cyrenian, who was coming in from the country, the father of Alexander and Rufus, to carry his cross.
Mark 15: 21

Moment of Silence

Leader: In the name of the Father
Today, an 86 year old man completed my diving certification course in Key West, FL. He said he wants his certification so he can dive at the Great Barrier Reef when he visits Australia in 2 weeks. "That sounds like fun. Are you a world traveler?" I asked. He laughed. "I was when I was your age. Actually, I was cleaning out an old filing cabinet yesterday. In it I found a list I made when I was 22 titled, '10 Things I Will Do Before I Die.' Diving at the Great Barrier Reef is #10 on the list, and it's the only one I haven't completed."

Moment of Silence

Leader: In the name of the Son
Today, my father found my little sister alive, chained up in a barn. She was abducted near Mexico City almost 5 months ago. Authorities stopped actively searching for her a few weeks later. My mother and I laid her soul to rest. We even had a funeral for her last month. All of our family and friends attended the ceremony except my father. He swore she was still alive. He looked for her all day, every day since she disappeared. And she's back home now because he never gave up.

Moment of Silence

Leader: In the name of the Holy Spirit
Today, my dad got home at 10AM after being overseas with the Army for almost 9 months. He took a taxi from the airport directly to the hospital. At noon my mom gave birth to my baby twin brothers.

All: Jesus our friend and brother, through your life and your journey to the cross, your death and resurrection, you have shown us how to live in love. May we always follow your example, living in redemption, living a life of compassion, in the search for peace through justice for all your people.

Station 9: Jesus Meets the Women of Jerusalem

Leader: We adore you, oh Christ, and we bless you.
All: **Because by your holy cross you have redeemed the world.**

Reading:

A large crowd of people followed Jesus, including many women who mourned and lamented him. Jesus turned to them and said, "Daughters of Jerusalem, do not weep for me; weep instead for yourselves and for your children, for indeed, the days are coming when people will say, 'Blessed are the barren, the wombs that never bore and the breasts that never nursed.' At that time, people will say to the mountains, 'Fall upon us!' and to the hills, 'Cover us!' for if these things are done when the wood is green what will happen when it is dry?"
Luke 23: 27-31

Moment of Silence

Leader: In the name of the Father
Today, I was eating breakfast inside a Chicago diner when I saw a homeless man out front have his money jar accidentally kicked over by one of the numerous people rushing by on the sidewalk. As a he scurried around trying to collect his money, the CEO of the company I work for stopped and helped him pick it all up. Then, when it was all collected, he reached into his wallet, pulled out a $20 bill, and stuffed it into the homeless man's jar.

Moment of Silence

Leader: In the name of the Son
Today, losing my infant son was the worst pain I have ever felt. But the phone call I just received from the doctor telling me my baby's organs instantly saved two other baby's lives.

Moment of Silence

Leader: In the name of the Holy Spirit
Today, a woman in my line at McDonald's noticed the uniformed Marine in line behind her, and when she handed me $20 to pay for her meal, she said, "Keep the extra $12 and use it to pay for the Marine's meal." When the Marine got up to the counter and ordered his food, I informed him that it was already paid for by another customer. He stared at me for a second, then turned his head and glanced out the front window, handed me his cash anyway and said, "Okay, make it two #4 meals then." On the way out of the restaurant he handed the second meal to the homeless man who was resting on the sidewalk.

All: Jesus our friend and brother, through your life and your journey to the cross, your death and resurrection, you have shown us how to live in love. May we always follow your example, living in redemption, living a life of compassion, in the search for peace through justice for all your people.

Station 10: Jesus is Crucified

Leader: We adore you, oh Christ, and we bless you.
All: **Because by your holy cross you have redeemed the world.**

Reading:

When they came to the place called the Skull, they crucified him and the criminals there, one on his right, the other on his left. [Then Jesus said, "Father, forgive them, they know not what they do."]
Luke 23: 33-34

Moment of Silence

Leader: In the name of the Father
Today, a local veteran firefighter's home was badly damaged in a fire that originated from faulty wiring. And sadly, his insurance only covers $10K of the $20K in damages. When word of this swept through the town, neighbors, friends, and total strangers (many of whom the firefighter assisted over the years) pooled money and resources and came up with the extra $10K and a month-long hotel stay to house his family while their house is being repaired.

Moment of Silence

Leader: In the name of the Son
Today at 9PM, in the Chinatown area of downtown Boston, I asked two teenagers for directions. They gave me the directions, but then insisted on walking with me to my destination. I was slightly suspicious of them until we were about halfway to my destination and I realized the neighborhood was not safe – an area a young woman should definitely not be in walking through by herself at night. And just as I was having this realization one of the teenagers said, "Now you see why we wanted to walk with you."

Moment of Silence

Leader: In the name of the Holy Spirit
Today, while my brother was drunk, he wrote a suicide note and posted it to his personal blog. An anonymous reader from California saw it a few minutes after he posted it, Goggled his home address and called the local police dispatch in Raleigh, NC. The paramedics found my brother unconscious on his bed with an empty Vicodin container next to him. They were able to pump his stomach and save his life.

All: Jesus our friend and brother, through your life and your journey to the cross, your death and resurrection, you have shown us how to live in love. May we always follow your example, living in redemption, living a life of compassion, in the search for peace through justice for all your people.

Station 11: Jesus Promises His Kingdom to the Good Thief

Leader: We adore you, oh Christ, and we bless you.
All: **Because by your holy cross you have redeemed the world.**

Reading:

 Now one of the criminals hanging there reviled Jesus, saying, "Are you not the Messiah? Save yourself and us." The other, however, rebuking him, said in reply, "Have you no fear of God, for you are subject to the same condemnation? And indeed, we have been condemned justly, for the sentence we received corresponds to our crimes, but this man has done nothing criminal." Then he said, "Jesus, remember me when you come into your kingdom." He replied to him, "Amen, I say to you, today you will be with me in Paradise."
Luke 23: 39-43

Moment of Silence

Leader: In the name of the Father
 Today, my dad passed away from natural causes at the age of 92. I found his body resting peacefully in the recliner in his bedroom. In his lap, facing upright, were three framed 8x10 photographs of my mom who passed away about 10 years ago. She was the love of his life, and apparently the last thing he wanted to see before he passed.

Moment of Silence

Leader: In the name of the Son
 Today, I am the proud mom of a blind 17-year-old boy. Although my son was born without his sense of sight, it hasn't stopped him from being a straight A student, a guitarist (whose band just surpassed 25,000 digital downloads of their first album), and an honest, loving boyfriend to his long-term girlfriend, Valerie. Just today, his younger sister asked him what he likes about Valerie, and he said, "Everything. She's beautiful."

Moment of Silence

Leader: In the name of the Holy Spirit
 Today, it's been a year since he passed away. But when I call my daughter in-law's house when she's not there, in the most chipper voice my late son answers and says, "Hi there! So glad you called, and sorry we missed ya! Please leave us a message." And it makes me cry every time. But I can't stop myself from listening to it.

All: Jesus our friend and brother, through your life and your journey to the cross, your death and resurrection, you have shown us how to live in love. May we always follow your example, living in redemption, living a life of compassion, in the search for peace through justice for all your people.

Station 12: Jesus Speaks to His Mother and the Disciple

Leader: We adore you, oh Christ, and we bless you.
All: **Because by your holy cross you have redeemed the world.**

Reading:

Standing by the cross of Jesus were his mother and his mother's sister, Mary the wife of Clopas, and Mary of Magdala. When Jesus saw his mother and the disciple there whom he loved, he said to his mother, "Woman, behold, your son." Then he said to the disciple, "Behold, your mother." And from that hour the disciple took her into his home.
John 19: 25-27

Moment of Silence

Leader: In the name of the Father
Today, it's been 10 years that our office janitor/maintenance man has been working at our company. Ever since he started, even as our small company grew from 12 people (when I started) to 118, he has given a small gift and card to every single one of his coworkers on their birthday. I actually just received my 10th gift and card from him last week. Today, for his birthday, the owner and CEO gave him a $25,000 bonus and threw him an after-work party.

Moment of Silence

Leader: In the name of the Son
Today, I'm a teacher in a low income neighborhood in greater Detroit. Because their parents don't have enough money, some of my students come to school without lunch, or without money for lunch. So I lend them a few dollars here and there to buy a school lunch when they are short on cash. I've been doing this for several years, and other teachers think I'm crazy. But of the few hundred dollars I've lent students over the years, I have received every single cent back. Sometimes it takes them a few weeks, but every one of my students has paid me back without me asking.

Moment of Silence

Leader: In the name of the Holy Spirit
Today before school, I confronted my friend about the scars on her arm and asked her why she cuts herself. She said, "All people cut for different reasons. I do it because I'd rather have scars on my arms than show the world the suffering on my face and the tears in my eyes." Without even thinking about it, I instantly hugged her tight for almost a full minute. When I finally let go, she had the most sincere smile on her face. This evening she texted me this: "I didn't cut myself at all today. I had no reason to. Thank you."

All: Jesus our friend and brother, through your life and your journey to the cross, your death and resurrection, you have shown us how to live in love. May we always follow your example, living in redemption, living a life of compassion, in the search for peace through justice for all your people.

Station 13: Jesus Dies on the Cross

Leader: We adore you, oh Christ, and we bless you.
All: **Because by your holy cross you have redeemed the world.**

Reading:

It was now about noon and darkness came over the whole land until three in the afternoon because of an eclipse of the sun. Then the veil of the temple was torn down the middle. Jesus cried out in a loud voice, "Father, into your hands I commend my spirit"; and when he had said this he breathed his last.
Luke 23: 44-46

Moment of Silence

Leader: In the name of the Father
Today, I left my journal at my school library, but went back to get it an hour later and it was still there. This evening I opened it to write, and on the last page, after my entry about my depression, someone wrote this: "Never give up. Ever. I've had my mom die from cancer. I've had a friend murdered. I've had a close friend commit suicide. I was almost deported last year. I used to hear, see and feel things that weren't there. But I'm still alive. After 17 years of struggle. After being abused, molested, and assaulted. After becoming addicted to self mutilation. I finally won. I beat my depression. And if I can, so can you. If I can live, then you can too. You're not alone."

Moment of Silence

Leader: In the name of the Son
Today, after I searched my apartment and determined it was lost, I picked up the phone to cancel my credit cards, and my doorbell rang. It was the homeless man who hangs out around the block. He smiled, held up my driver's license and said, "I recognized your picture. You are one of the few people who has given me clothes, blankets and leftovers over the years. I figured this was my opportunity to give back." He handed me my wallet with everything intact, including $86 in cash.

Moment of Silence

Leader: In the name of the Holy Spirit
Today, I am a nurse at the general hospital in my hometown. This evening our old class of 2000 prom queen was rushed to the hospital after a car accident. The surgeon that worked on her relentlessly the entire evening until she was in stable condition was once the quiet boy who I vividly remember her mercilessly teasing all four years of high school.

All: Jesus our friend and brother, through your life and your journey to the cross, your death and resurrection, you have shown us how to live in love. May we always follow your example, living in redemption, living a life of compassion, in the search for peace through justice for all your people.

Station 14: Jesus is Placed in the Tomb

Leader: We adore you, oh Christ, and we bless you.
All: **Because by your holy cross you have redeemed the world.**

Reading:

When it was evening, there came a rich man from Arimathea named Joseph, who was himself a disciple of Jesus. He went to Pilate and asked for the body of Jesus; then Pilate ordered it to be handed over. Taking the body, Joseph wrapped it [in] clean linen and laid it in his new tomb that he had hewn in the rock. Then he rolled a huge stone across the entrance to the tomb and departed.
Matthew 27: 57-60

Moment of Silence

Leader: In the name of the Father
Today, I came across a Facebook page with 89 fans that's dedicated to making fun of a kid at my school. It made me sick to my stomach. So I wrote this on the page's wall: "Read your cruel words, and then get up and look in the mirror, all of you! And say, 'I like torturing others! I am proud of myself!'" I just checked the Facebook page again, about 7 hours later. No one responded to my post. But the page now has 26 fans.

Moment of Silence

Leader: In the name of the Son
Today, I was sitting on the subway, exhausted, in a horrible mood. Lately I just haven't been happy. I've been struggling with my weight, my job, and life in general. About 15 minutes into the subway ride, the elderly lady across from me got up, moved next to me, and said, "You're beautiful. I'm not joking. I was thinking it, and I wanted you to know." I smiled, thanked her and asked, "Do you usually complement strangers?" "When I was your age, a woman my age sat next to me on a train. Her compliments saved me from doing something stupid. And today, I'm returning the favor."

Moment of Silence

Leader: In the name of the Holy Spirit
Today, I operated on a little girl that was in a car accident. She desperately needed O- blood, which is a bit rare. We didn't have any available, but her twin brother was at the hospital who had O- blood. I explained to him that it was a matter of life and death – that his sister needed his blood. He sat quietly for a moment, and then said goodbye to his parents. I didn't think anything of it until after we took the blood we needed and he asked, "So when will I die?" He thought he was giving his life for hers. Thankfully, they'll both be fine.

All: Jesus our friend and brother, through your life and your journey to the cross, your death and resurrection, you have shown us how to live in love. May we always follow your example, living in redemption, living a life of compassion, in the search for peace through justice for all your people.

Moment of Silence

"**Darkness cannot drive out darkness,**

only light can do that.

Hate cannot drive out hate;

only love can do that".

-Rev. Dr. Martin Luther King, Jr.

Leader:

 Holy Trinity, we ask that you forgive us for the wrongs that we have done against each other. We ask that you guide us to recognize and help us when others are in time of need, and for others to help us in those times. We ask and pray that we lead a life that is positive for you and for your universe. We ask and pray that we can be leading examples of your goodness towards others and towards ourselves. We thank you for those that you have brought into this world that have examples to us of the way that we should help and treat not only ourselves, also but others, and that we may follow in their example in Loving our neighbor as ourselves.

We thank you for those who have worked hard against Racism, Sexism, Homophobia, Classism, and for all of the other wrongs that we have done against each other.

Leader: Forgive us for remaining silent and bound by fear
All: Give us courage to speak and act with justice

Leader: Forgive us our arrogance in closing our eyes to other peoples and cultures
All: Forgive us for disfiguring this land and despoiling its bounty

Leader: Forgive us for despising the cultures of others, and taking away their self-respect
All: Give us grace to bind one anothers wounds

Leader: Forgive us for not listening to the griefs of all who are oppressed in this land
All: Draw us together as one people

Leader: Forgive us for our prejudice and indifference towards those whose ways are different from our ways
All: Strengthen us to live with respect and compassion for one another

(All turn and fast each other in a circle if possible)

All:
 I ask you my brothers and sisters in Christ, for forgiveness for the wrongs that I have done in the past towards you. From this time on, I will do my best to do no injustices towards all that I am with, and to be a shining example of the Love that the Holy Trinity has for us all.

Leader:
We are the body of Christ

All:
His spirit is with us

Leader:
May the Peace of the Lord be Always with you.

All:
And also with you.

(If this is being done in a church and/or a clergy person is present, Holy Communion <u>can</u> be held beginning here)

Leader:
Go in Peace to love and serve the Lord

All:
Thanks be to God.

Leader:
As you leave, please greet each other in the Peace.

Stations Of The Cross

I Am Asking For Forgiveness

By Earl Clinton Williams, Jr.

<u>Acclamations</u>

What you are about to read and listen to is about Forgiveness. Are you ready to Forgive or be Forgiven, but more importantly to be able to Forgive Yourself?

I would like to thank my parents, my sister, my nephews, my relatives, friends, the Episcopal Church, and the Quakers, along with many others who helped me become the person that I am.

I would also like to give thanks to the Holy Trinity in guiding me through the process of putting this together. I only hope and pray that this is an instrument that will help this world become a better place.

Station 1: Jesus in the Garden of Gethsemane

-

Leader: We adore you, oh Christ, and we bless you.
All: **Because by your holy cross you have redeemed the world.**

Reading:

Then Jesus came with them to a place called Gethsemane, and he said to his disciples, "Sit here while I go over there and pray." He took along Peter and the two sons of Zebedee, and began to feel sorrow and distress. Then he said to them, "My soul is sorrowful even to death. Remain here and keep watch with me." He advanced a little and fell prostrate in prayer, saying, "My Father, if it is possible, let this cup pass from me; yet, not as I will, but as you will." When he returned to his disciples he found them asleep. He said to Peter, "So you could not keep watch with me for one hour? Watch and pray that you may not undergo the test. The spirit is willing, but the flesh is weak."
Matthew 25:36-41

Moment of Silence

Story:

When I have wronged others, I humble myself and admit it. It strengthens bonds and cements friendships. Unless the wrong has crushed and destroyed. Sometimes it's difficult for us to do, but that is because pride is ruling as king. It takes strength and chutzpah to admit when we are wrong. But it makes us free and happy that we have. We all make mistakes and not one of us doesn't. On the other hand. when someone commits a mistake that affects us, then we should show mercy and forgive them, too. Especially when they are sorry for doing it. We are in this thing together.

Moment of Silence

All: Living, loving Spirit, let me practice forgiveness today by starting with the little hurts. I will let go of all the everyday occurrences that do not go the way I want, and the moment I begin to feel the familiar feeling of anger or resentment, I will practice forgiveness by invoking your loving and peaceful Presence and allowing divine grace to surround me. And so it is..

Station 2: Jesus, Betrayed by Judas, is Arrested

Leader: We adore you, oh Christ, and we bless you.
All: **Because by your holy cross you have redeemed the world.**

Reading:

Then, while [Jesus] was still speaking, Judas, one of the Twelve, arrived, accompanied by a crowd with swords and clubs, who had come from the chief priests, the scribes, and the elders. His betrayer had arranged a signal with them, saying, "the man I shall kiss is the one; arrest him and lead him away securely." He came and immediately went over to him and said, "Rabbi." And he kissed him. At this they laid hands on him and arrested him.
Mark 14: 43-46

Moment of Silence

Story:

When we have wronged someone, it is always the right thing to do and apologize. It makes for better relationships and a clean conscience. I have never had a problem doing that. My conscience doesn't allow me to know that I have offended or hurt someone and not apologize. Sometimes even after they have accepted my apology, I will feel really bad and beat myself up with it. I have since learned what not to do to cause these apologies to have to happen. And I'm going to be more cognizant of this in the future.

Moment of Silence

All: Living, loving Spirit, let me practice forgiveness today by starting with the little hurts. I will let go of all the everyday occurrences that do not go the way I want, and the moment I begin to feel the familiar feeling of anger or resentment, I will practice forgiveness by invoking your loving and peaceful Presence and allowing divine grace to surround me. And so it is.

Station 3: Jesus is Condemned by the Sanhedrin

Leader: We adore you, oh Christ, and we bless you.
All: **Because by your holy cross you have redeemed the world.**

Reading:

When day came the council of elders of the people met, both chief priests and scribes, and they brought him before their Sanhedrin. They said, "If you are the Messiah, tell us," but he replied to them, "If I tell you, you will not believe, and if I question, you will not respond. But from this time on the Son of Man will be seated at the right hand of the power of God." They all asked, "Are you then the Son of God?" He replied to them, "You say that I am." Then they said, "What further need have we for testimony? We have heard it from his own mouth."
Luke 22: 66-71

Moment of Silence

Story:

I am not too big, too arrogant or ignorant to say Sorry when I have wronged you As you mature, grow and find out who you are as a person, you also realize how important the word 'Sorry' is - its sadly over used, and under appreciated....

But when used correctly, with the right sincerity and emotion and contrition, then apologies and the word mean the right thing to the wronged person....

Moment of Silence

All: Living, loving Spirit, let me practice forgiveness today by starting with the little hurts. I will let go of all the everyday occurrences that do not go the way I want, and the moment I begin to feel the familiar feeling of anger or resentment, I will practice forgiveness by invoking your loving and peaceful Presence and allowing divine grace to surround me. And so it is..

Station 4: Jesus is Denied by Peter

Leader: We adore you, oh Christ, and we bless you.
All: **Because by your holy cross you have redeemed the world.**

Reading:

Now Peter was sitting outside in the courtyard. One of the maids came over to him and said, "You too were with Jesus the Galilean." But he denied it in front of everyone, saying, "I do not know what you are talking about!" As he went out to the gate, another girl saw him and said to those who were there, "This man was with Jesus the Nazorean." Again he denied it with an oath, "I do not know the man!" A little later the bystanders came over and said to Peter, "Surely you too are one of them; even your speech gives you away." At that he began to curse and to swear, "I do not know the man." And immediately a cock crowed. Then Peter remembered the word that Jesus had spoken: "Before the cock crows you will deny me three times." He went out and began to weep bitterly.
Matthew 26: 69-75

Moment of Silence

Story:

If you do not forgive, you may get in the way of the work God is trying to do in the other person's life.

"Early in my divorce process," says Laura Petherbridge, "I was thinking of people I know who have gone through divorce and years later are still very bitter. I prayed, 'God, I don't want to end up a bitter woman, but I don't know how to let it go because the hurt is so deep. Please show me how to resolve this resentment.'

"I learned to pray for the 'other woman,' which probably seems like an impossible thing. It was not by my own strength. Something deep within me knew my own healing would come. I asked God to help me to see her as He views her. I began to see her as a lost person who believed that taking another woman's husband would make her feel better about herself. She was no longer my enemy, but instead an empty woman without God in her life. The bitterness began to melt away."

When you forgive, you allow God to work in the other person's life. Choosing to walk in obedience has a net positive effect on you and on people around you. Keep persevering in prayer for those who have hurt you. As Paul says in Philippians, "Keep pressing on."

"Brothers, I do not consider myself yet to have taken hold of it. But one thing I do: Forgetting what is behind and straining toward what is ahead, I press on toward the goal to win the prize for which God has called me heavenward in Christ Jesus" (Philippians 3:13-14).

Moment of Silence

All: Living, loving Spirit, let me practice forgiveness today by starting with the little hurts. I will let go of all the everyday occurrences that do not go the way I want, and the moment I begin to feel the familiar feeling of anger or resentment, I will practice forgiveness by invoking your loving and peaceful Presence and allowing divine grace to surround me. And so it is..

Station 5: Jesus is Judged by Pilate

Leader: We adore you, oh Christ, and we bless you.
All: **Because by your holy cross you have redeemed the world.**

Reading:

The chief priests with the elders and the scribes, that is, the whole Sanhedrin, held a council. They bound Jesus, led him away, and handed him over to Pilate. Pilate questioned him, "Are you the king of the Jews?" He said to him in reply, "You say so." The chief priests accused him of many things. Again Pilate questioned him, "Have you no answer? See how many things they accuse you of." Jesus gave him no further answer, so that Pilate was amazed.... Pilate, wishing to satisfy the crowd, released Barrabas... [and] handed [Jesus] over to be crucified.
Mark 15: 1-5, 15

Moment of Silence

Story:

Where would we be without forgiveness? I dare say we wouldn't have any friends, relationships with family would be dead. I mean everyone does something to you that takes forgiveness. The world would be consumed with war. That would definitely not be a place I would want to live. I believe in forgiveness all the way, though sometimes I do feel like it might be necessary to teach a lesson or two

Moment of Silence

All: Living, loving Spirit, let me practice forgiveness today by starting with the little hurts. I will let go of all the everyday occurrences that do not go the way I want, and the moment I begin to feel the familiar feeling of anger or resentment, I will practice forgiveness by invoking your loving and peaceful Presence and allowing divine grace to surround me. And so it is..

Station 6: Jesus is Scourged and Crowned with Thorns

Leader: We adore you, oh Christ, and we bless you.

All: **Because by your holy cross you have redeemed the world.**

Reading:

Then Pilate took Jesus and had him scourged. And the soldiers wove a crown out of thorns and placed it on his head, and clothed him in a purple cloak, and they came to him and said,"Hail, King of the Jews!" And they struck him repeatedly.

John 19: 1-3

Moment of Silence

For a number of years I have been involved at a place where it seems that I get tested a large number of times with my ability to forgive people over and over. I get to hear excuses over and over about things instead of hearing an apology about things done to me and/or others, but that rarely happens. I get to hear about how things are more important for others to get what they want over the things that I desire. Then with some things that I do they get upset and angry with me and tell me how wrong I am and expect for me to apologize. I have spent hours and days working on things only to see the credit be given to others, and when I have said something, instead of hearing "I'm sorry", I hear excuses. I have gone out into the larger community and have had to listen to complaints about people within the place, and even people within the place come to me with their complaints. Having to deal with the stuff that has gone on has gotten to my health, and I have gone to bed crying over the way that I get treated. But the funny thing is that they feel that I am one of the few people that they can rely on. Yes I should leave, and in fact had planned to several years ago but had been asked by those who knew that I was planning over leaving to stay, as they like the fact that I will apologize and/or ask for forgiveness with things when I have been clearly wrong.

It took me a while to be able to forgive those who just seem to want to use, abuse and hurt me by their actions of the past and now, but I know that in the end the only people that they are really hurting is themselves. I realize that they really need to deal with their own hurts from the past and hopefully one day will learn to not only forgive those that have hurt them in the past, but might one day ask for forgiveness from those that they hurt without giving excuses.

But most importantly I am learning how to forgive myself for the wrongs that I have done and am even laughing inside at those who treat me wrong for they are in reality only hurting themselves.

Moment of Silence

All: Living, loving Spirit, let me practice forgiveness today by starting with the little hurts. I will let go of all the everyday occurrences that do not go the way I want, and the moment I begin to feel the familiar feeling of anger or resentment, I will practice forgiveness by invoking your loving and peaceful Presence and allowing divine grace to surround me. And so it is..

Station 7: Jesus Bears the Cross

Leader: We adore you, oh Christ, and we bless you.
All: **Because by your holy cross you have redeemed the world.**

Reading:

When the chief priests and the guards saw [Jesus] they cried out, "Crucify him, crucify him!" Pilate said to them, "Take him yourselves and crucify him. I find no guilt in him." ... They cried out, "Take him away, take him away! Crucify him!" Pilate said to them, "Shall I crucify your king?" The chief priests answered, "We have no king but Caesar." Then he handed him over to them to be crucified. So they took Jesus, and carrying the cross himself he went out to what is called the Place of the Skull, in Hebrew,Golgotha.
John 19: 6, 15-17

Moment of Silence

Story:

I believe that people make mistakes. Sometimes, those can harm you or intrude on your life. You need to understand that sometimes there are things that you need to just accept and move on with your life.

Take, for example, road rage. If somebody cuts you off in traffic, you should just let it roll off your shoulders...don't let it bug you. Just forgive them - if you accidentally cut somebody off, wouldn't you want to be forgiven?

Try to put your past behind you...forgive the transgressions others have committed against you, in the hopes that others can forget those you've caused against them.

Moment of Silence

All: Living, loving Spirit, let me practice forgiveness today by starting with the little hurts. I will let go of all the everyday occurrences that do not go the way I want, and the moment I begin to feel the familiar feeling of anger or resentment, I will practice forgiveness by invoking your loving and peaceful Presence and allowing divine grace to surround me. And so it is.

Station 8: Jesus is Helped by Simon the Cyrenian to Carry the Cross

Leader: We adore you, oh Christ, and we bless you.
All: **Because by your holy cross you have redeemed the world.**

Reading:

They pressed into service a passer-by, Simon, a Cyrenian, who was coming in from the country, the father of Alexander and Rufus, to carry his cross.
Mark 15: 21

Moment of Silence

Story:

Be kind to yourself and you will find it natural to be kind to others. Forgive others and you will naturally forgive yourself. This is the essence of happiness. It is liberating to recognize that we are connected in spirit and identity with those who hurt us and with all others who make poor choices. Maybe that is why Eastern philosophers focus on being one with everything. Maybe that is why Jesus said "Forgiveness covereth a multitude of sins." He chose willingly to take the sins of humanity upon himself. Someone else wrote, "Forgiveness is to set a prisoner free and to discover that the prisoner was you."

Moment of Silence

All: Living, loving Spirit, let me practice forgiveness today by starting with the little hurts. I will let go of all the everyday occurrences that do not go the way I want, and the moment I begin to feel the familiar feeling of anger or resentment, I will practice forgiveness by invoking your loving and peaceful Presence and allowing divine grace to surround me. And so it is.

Station 9: Jesus Meets the Women of Jerusalem

Leader: We adore you, oh Christ, and we bless you.
All: **Because by your holy cross you have redeemed the world.**

Reading:

A large crowd of people followed Jesus, including many women who mourned and lamented him. Jesus turned to them and said, "Daughters of Jerusalem, do not weep for me; weep instead for yourselves and for your children, for indeed, the days are coming when people will say, 'Blessed are the barren, the wombs that never bore and the breasts that never nursed.' At that time, people will say to the mountains, 'Fall upon us!' and to the hills, 'Cover us!' for if these things are done when the wood is green what will happen when it is dry?"
Luke 23: 27-31

Moment of Silence

Story:

Have you ever been SO PISSED at someone that you SWORE you would never ever talk to them, or forgive them for what they've done? I have. It creates bitterness, hurt, stabbing hearts.

I learned so much. Growing older definitely is a plus, in this way.

When people forgive, they release that anger and hurt from their heart. Its like a burden that is lifted. **"Be kind and loving to each other, and forgive each other just as God has forgave you in Christ.**
Ephesians 4:32
That doesn't necessarily mean that you have to be there best friend, but forgiving is the first step in peace and happiness that God wants for our lives. I find it simply easier to forgive anyway. Hate is a harsh nasty word **AND FEELING**

Moment of Silence   .

All: Living, loving Spirit, let me practice forgiveness today by starting with the little hurts. I will let go of all the everyday occurrences that do not go the way I want, and the moment I begin to feel the familiar feeling of anger or resentment, I will practice forgiveness by invoking your loving and peaceful Presence and allowing divine grace to surround me. And so it is..

Station 10: Jesus is Crucified

Leader: We adore you, oh Christ, and we bless you.
All: **Because by your holy cross you have redeemed the world.**

Reading:

When they came to the place called the Skull, they crucified him and the criminals there, one on his right, the other on his left. [Then Jesus said, "Father, forgive them, they know not what they do."] *Luke 23: 33-34*

Moment of Silence

Story:

Forgiveness is a gift we give to others as well as ourselves.

We all have our reasons for doing the wrongs we have done to others. Likewise we have beliefs or perceptions of wrongs done to us and why. We cannot see into the heart and mind of those we are at odds with. Their reasoning for their part can be just as valid as our own.

If we do not forgive someone for something then we are likely to retaliate in kind and the cycle continues. Someone has to stand up and be forgiving of the other and put an end to the madness of retribution.

An eye for an eye? But, do two wrongs make a right? I think not.

Forgiving others and putting things behind us can be a very freeing experience. You may not wish to continue a relationship with a person who has wronged you, but forgiving them and moving on is important. Letting go of the past and the resentments we carry due to lack of forgiveness, frees our hearts and minds to deal with the present and to look to the future.

So if there is someone out there that you have not made peace with... maybe it's been so long that you don't even know what happened... try forgiving and letting go. It is amazing what a difference it can make.

Moment of Silence

All: Living, loving Spirit, let me practice forgiveness today by starting with the little hurts. I will let go of all the everyday occurrences that do not go the way I want, and the moment I begin to feel the familiar feeling of anger or resentment, I will practice forgiveness by invoking your loving and peaceful Presence and allowing divine grace to surround me. And so it is..

Station 11: Jesus Promises His Kingdom to the Good Thief

Leader: We adore you, oh Christ, and we bless you.
All: **Because by your holy cross you have redeemed the world.**

Reading:

Now one of the criminals hanging there reviled Jesus, saying, "Are you not the Messiah? Save yourself and us." The other, however, rebuking him, said in reply, "Have you no fear of God, for you are subject to the same condemnation? And indeed, we have been condemned justly, for the sentence we received corresponds to our crimes, but this man has done nothing criminal." Then he said, "Jesus, remember me when you come into your kingdom." He replied to him, "Amen, I say to you, today you will be with me in Paradise."
Luke 23: 39-43

Moment of Silence

Story:

To forgive
Is not to forget.

To forgive
Is really to remember
That nobody is perfect

That each of us stumbles
When we want so much to stay upright

That each of us says things
We wish we had never said

That we can all forget that love
Is more important than being right.

To forgive
Is really to remember
That we are so much more
Than our mistakes

That we are often more kind and caring
That accepting anothers' flaws
Can help us accept our own.

To forgive

Is to remember

That the odds are pretty good that

We might soon need to be forgiven ourselves.

That life sometimes gives us more

Than we can handle gracefully.

To forgive

Is to remember

That we have room in our hearts to

Begin again

And again,

And again.

~ By Mestup Poems

Moment of Silence

All: Living, loving Spirit, let me practice forgiveness today by starting with the little hurts. I will let go of all the everyday occurrences that do not go the way I want, and the moment I begin to feel the familiar feeling of anger or resentment, I will practice forgiveness by invoking your loving and peaceful Presence and allowing divine grace to surround me. And so it is..

Station 12: Jesus Speaks to His Mother and the Disciple

Leader: We adore you, oh Christ, and we bless you.
All: **Because by your holy cross you have redeemed the world.**

Reading:

Standing by the cross of Jesus were his mother and his mother's sister, Mary the wife of Clopas, and Mary of Magdala. When Jesus saw his mother and the disciple there whom he loved, he said to his mother, "Woman, behold, your son." Then he said to the disciple, "Behold, your mother." And from that hour the disciple took her into his home.
John 19: 25-27

Moment of Silence

Story:

Forgiveness isn't about the other guy. It's about me.

It's about me carrying around a load of anger and hatred and misery...while most of the time, the other person hasn't a clue. Or if they do, they don't give a damn.

Those emotions, that hate, anger, all of it, drain *my* energy, but do nothing to deal with the person they are aimed at. I could wind up with ulcers and migraine headaches, but the person I'm hating has no effects at all.

So I choose to forgive.

Not for their sakes, but for mine. I don't want to carry all this baggage around.

So I forgive.

Moment of Silence

All: Living, loving Spirit, let me practice forgiveness today by starting with the little hurts. I will let go of all the everyday occurrences that do not go the way I want, and the moment I begin to feel the familiar feeling of anger or resentment, I will practice forgiveness by invoking your loving and peaceful Presence and allowing divine grace to surround me. And so it is..

Station 13: Jesus Dies on the Cross

Leader: We adore you, oh Christ, and we bless you.
All: **Because by your holy cross you have redeemed the world.**

Reading:

It was now about noon and darkness came over the whole land until three in the afternoon because of an eclipse of the sun. Then the veil of the temple was torn down the middle. Jesus cried out in a loud voice, "Father, into your hands I commend my spirit"; and when he had said this he breathed his last. *Luke 23: 44-46*

Moment of Silence

Story:

You have to be forgiveful. The human nation is suppose to make mistakes and bad decisions. It is apart of growing up. No one can truly say that they have never done something bad. Just forgive and forget and you will keep living in the past. You might need that person one day or they might need you. Don't let anger stop anything. It is a stupid emotion

Moment of Silence

All: Living, loving Spirit, let me practice forgiveness today by starting with the little hurts. I will let go of all the everyday occurrences that do not go the way I want, and the moment I begin to feel the familiar feeling of anger or resentment, I will practice forgiveness by invoking your loving and peaceful Presence and allowing divine grace to surround me. And so it is.

Station 14: Jesus is Placed in the Tomb

Leader: We adore you, oh Christ, and we bless you.
All: **Because by your holy cross you have redeemed the world.**

Reading:

When it was evening, there came a rich man from Arimathea named Joseph, who was himself a disciple of Jesus. He went to Pilate and asked for the body of Jesus; then Pilate ordered it to be handed over. Taking the body, Joseph wrapped it [in] clean linen and laid it in his new tomb that he had hewn in the rock. Then he rolled a huge stone across the entrance to the tomb and departed. *Matthew 27: 57-60*

Moment of Silence

Story:

Wikipedia defines forgiveness as the "mental and/or spiritual process of ceasing to feel resentment, indignation or anger against another person for a perceived offense of mistake."

I think that perceived is a key word here. My step father left my mother when she was 64 for a 56 year old...he was 72. My mom died less than a year later....I blamed him.

I perceived he did wrong and he doesn't. Therefore he feels he has done nothing wrong for me to forgive. It would be easier to forgive him if he apologized for the hurt but I know that won't happen.

So realizing this, I know that forgiveness is a gift I have to give myself. A release from the anger and the past, allowing me to go forward with my life and my dreams.

In this same light, I need to forgive my husband for all the past hurts. I hope we can mend our relationship.

Whether they deserve to be forgiven is no longer an issue for me. I will do it for myself to free me from the debilitating energy drain of holding on to my resentments and allowing their past actions to continue to hurt me.

I don't want to define myself by my past hurts. I will work on this process and like the clean spring rain, clear the pollution away.

Moment of Silence

All: Living, loving Spirit, let me practice forgiveness today by starting with the little hurts. I will let go of all the everyday occurrences that do not go the way I want, and the moment I begin to feel the familiar feeling of anger or resentment, I will practice forgiveness by invoking your loving and peaceful Presence and allowing divine grace to surround me. And so it is..

The Lord's Prayer

Our Father, which art in heaven,
Hallowed be thy Name.
Thy Kingdom come.
Thy will be done on earth,
As it is in heaven.
Give us this day our daily bread.
And forgive us our trespasses,
As we forgive them that trespass against us.
And lead us not into temptation,
But deliver us from evil.
For thine is the kingdom,
The power, and the glory,
For ever and ever.
Amen.

The Apostles' Creed

I believe in God, the Father Almighty,
the Maker of heaven and earth,
and in Jesus Christ, His only Son, our Lord:
Who was conceived by the Holy Ghost,
born of the virgin Mary,
suffered under Pontius Pilate,
was crucified, dead, and buried;
He descended into hell.
The third day He arose again from the dead;
He ascended into heaven,
and sitteth on the right hand of God the Father Almighty;
from thence he shall come to judge the quick and the dead.
I believe in the Holy Ghost;
the holy catholic church;
the communion of saints;
the forgiveness of sins;
the resurrection of the body;
and the life everlasting.
Amen.

Stations Of The Cross

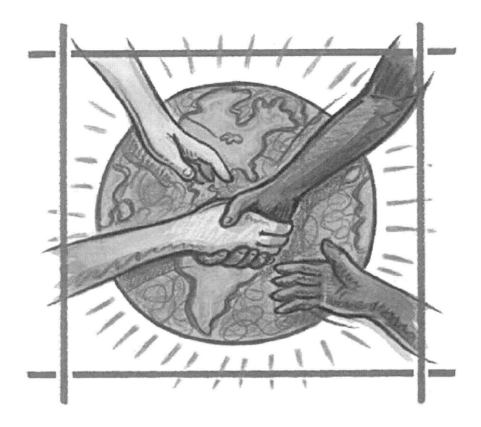

Let's Talk About Race II

By Earl Clinton Williams, Jr.

<u>Acclamations</u>

Except for this paragraph, the rest of this acclamation remains the same. The only thing that I have changed in this version are the stories. I hope that these stories will be a benefit and meaningful to you and the world.

What you are about to read and experience will hopefully make you think about Race and Racism and how you can help to not only help the world to become a place where this subject will become a thing of the past, but it will hopefully help you into making better choices in the way that you treat others of different colors, nationalities, ethnic groups, and much more in a better way. Hopefully this will make you realize that no matter how much you may deny that you are a racist, you will realize that EVERYBODY has a bit of it in them. Many people look and think that it's those who are in such groups as the KKK and Nazis that are racist, but even those who think that they are on the total opposite end of that kind of thinking do racist things themselves.

I would like to give big thanks to my friends and family, the people on The Experience Project (http://www.experienceproject.com, and others who's stories that are within these pages. I would like to give a special thanks to damili ayo, one of my favorite authors and one of the best social justice advocates that this world has toward working for equality for all. I would like to give thanks to ALL that have died fighting for equality for all. most importantly I would like to thank my parents, sister, nephews, grandparent, the Quakers, The Episcopal Church, the people of Grace Epiphany Episcopal Church in Philadelphia, Pa. and others who have helped me to understand that there is more to people than the color of their skin.

I would also like to give thanks to the Holy Trinity in guiding me through the process of putting this together. I only hope and pray that this is an instrument that will help this world become a better place.

Station 1: Jesus in the Garden of Gethsemane

Leader: We adore you, oh Christ, and we bless you.
All: **Because by your holy cross you have redeemed the world.**

Reading:

Then Jesus came with them to a place called Gethsemane, and he said to his disciples, "Sit here while I go over there and pray." He took along Peter and the two sons of Zebedee, and began to feel sorrow and distress. Then he said to them, "My soul is sorrowful even to death. Remain here and keep watch with me." He advanced a little and fell prostrate in prayer, saying, "My Father, if it is possible, let this cup pass from me; yet, not as I will, but as you will." When he returned to his disciples he found them asleep. He said to Peter, "So you could not keep watch with me for one hour? Watch and pray that you may not undergo the test. The spirit is willing, but the flesh is weak."
Matthew 25:36-41

Moment of Silence

Story:

Bad Body Shop Experience

I went to The Body Shop in Yorkdale. When I went inside, a White woman approached me. She seemed kind and asked what I was looking for. I told her I was just taking a look at the products. She understood, and went on her way. As I was looking around, I noticed a Chinese woman behind the counter. When she saw me, she immediately rushed towards me. She asked me what I was looking for and I told her the same thing I told the other woman. This time though, she wouldn't leave me be. I obviously knew she was following me throughout the store. Wherever I went, she went. My brother felt really uncomfortable with the situation and said he would wait outside. As I was browsing along the store, I saw some girls in there with me. The only difference was, nobody was following them. I totally knew it. It's because I'm a visible minority! After realizing that was the reason I was being followed, I left.

I was so shocked. I couldn't believe it. I was being followed because of the colour of my skin. I only see this things happen on T.V, but I didn't expect that to happen to me. The other thing that shocked me most was that the woman following me was a visible minority too! Honestly, If I were to know that I would be followed, I would of thought the White woman in the store would follow me, not the Asian woman. I think that most of the time, visible ethnicity's are far more racist towards one another then White people are towards us. It's sad, but true.

I didn't purchase anything in the store, but I probably will just because I love The Body Shop's products. If this does happen again though, I will definitely speak up and I'll let you guys know how It went.

Moment of Silence

All: Jesus our friend and brother, through your life and your journey to the cross, your death and resurrection, you have shown us how to live in love. May we always follow your example, living in redemption, living a life of compassion, in the search for peace through justice for all your people.

Station 2: Jesus, Betrayed by Judas, is Arrested

Leader: We adore you, oh Christ, and we bless you.
All: **Because by your holy cross you have redeemed the world.**

Reading:

Then, while [Jesus] was still speaking, Judas, one of the Twelve, arrived, accompanied by a crowd with swords and clubs, who had come from the chief priests, the scribes, and the elders. His betrayer had arranged a signal with them, saying, "the man I shall kiss is the one; arrest him and lead him away securely." He came and immediately went over to him and said, "Rabbi." And he kissed him. At this they laid hands on him and arrested him.
Mark 14: 43-46

Moment of Silence

Story:

Being At Work Sucks...

So I have face a LOT of Racism at work but it happened again yesterday and I am just pissed off.
I work at a radio station and the sales manager and a sales rep were standing outside of the studio I was working in talking about a client of theirs which happens to be one of the local tribes. The sales manager did that "wo-wo-wo-wo" thing on his mouth that people do and the sales guy said that they were going to go out there to collect their money because "they don't trust no damn Indian" so I yelled "come-on guys!" at them and closed my door so that I would not have to listen to it anymore.

The Sales Manager came in later and told me he was not disrespectful and that I should remember that and he said that he DID not say anything wrong and did I get that? I am guessing he was saying "don't sue us" more than sorry.

At least it was not as bad as the time I was talking to two of the sales guys and one of them said that All American Indians were just pissed off because all they have are moccasin and stupid beads and they have to see all the successful white people who are actually making something of themselves and they are jealous. I said "hey, I am American Indian, can't you tell by looking at me?" and he said "Oh well you should know than." I went on to say that I had gone to college and worked hard for what I have and he said "they only reason you went to or passed college is because you got it paid for by scholarships and affirmative action." which is a load of CRAP. The only Scholarship I got was a merit Scholarship because the tribes I belong to are BROKE and don't offer money for school.

I digress... and don't even get me STARTED on the sexism that I have to put up with every day at my job. I can't wait to leave!! I almost never get mad and it takes a lot and I can laugh off a lot but I think I am hitting my limit.

Moment of Silence

All: Jesus our friend and brother, through your life and your journey to the cross, your death and resurrection, you have shown us how to live in love. May we always follow your example, living in redemption, living a life of compassion, in the search for peace through justice for all your people.

Station 3: Jesus is Condemned by the Sanhedrin

Leader: We adore you, oh Christ, and we bless you.
All: **Because by your holy cross you have redeemed the world.**

Reading:

When day came the council of elders of the people met, both chief priests and scribes, and they brought him before their Sanhedrin. They said, "If you are the Messiah, tell us," but he replied to them, "If I tell you, you will not believe, and if I question, you will not respond. But from this time on the Son of Man will be seated at the right hand of the power of God." They all asked, "Are you then the Son of God?" He replied to them, "You say that I am." Then they said, "What further need have we for testimony? We have heard it from his own mouth."
Luke 22: 66-71

Moment of Silence

Story:

No matter if you believe in the Big Bang Theory, that we all evolved from apes, or that we were made in the Image of God, one thing is for certain. We all no matter our race, came here or came to be a breathing life form the same way as everyone else did.

Race should not matter, but in America it really does. Everything matters in America. Your religion, your sex, whether or not you're gay, etc, I could go on. Sadly to say, I thought that race mattered in every corner of the Earth. But from learning Spanish, I have come to know that only in America and the UK, race and other differences separate all of their inhabitants on one form or another. In most Spanish speaking countries, people are usually just treated the same, they only judge the tongue you speak.

Its sad that so many people had to die for basic rights because they were born with a certain tint to their skin, or because they choose to call God - Allah, or couldn't give an opinion that mattered on something just because of their sex.

Why should my race determine what neighborhood I visit?... Why should my race and gender depict what other races think of me (in the media)?... Why can't I be something else other than Christian?...

In 2000 and beyond, there should be no discussion about race. There should only be question about a person's heart, their actions, their character.

Moment of Silence

All: Jesus our friend and brother, through your life and your journey to the cross, your death and resurrection, you have shown us how to live in love. May we always follow your example, living in redemption, living a life of compassion, in the search for peace through justice for all your people.

Station 4: Jesus is Denied by Peter

Leader: We adore you, oh Christ, and we bless you.
All: **Because by your holy cross you have redeemed the world.**

Reading:

Now Peter was sitting outside in the courtyard. One of the maids came over to him and said, "You too were with Jesus the Galilean." But he denied it in front of everyone, saying, "I do not know what you are talking about!" As he went out to the gate, another girl saw him and said to those who were there, "This man was with Jesus the Nazorean." Again he denied it with an oath, "I do not know the man!" A little later the bystanders came over and said to Peter, "Surely you too are one of them; even your speech gives you away." At that he began to curse and to swear, "I do not know the man." And immediately a cock crowed. Then Peter remembered the word that Jesus had spoken: "Before the cock crows you will deny me three times." He went out and began to weep bitterly.
Matthew 26: 69-75

Moment of Silence

Story:

I grew up in the 60s near Plainfield, NJ where the infamous riots after ML Kings assassination took place right outside my grandmothers door.

My parents were extremely racist which spread to my siblings and I. The N word was used daily. To be called a N was worse than being called a retard, whore, b. We had to lock our doors and windows at night so the "n" didn't get us. We had to lock our car doors when crossing over the bridge into Plainfield so those "animals" wouldn't attack us. And we finally had to move out of our town when I was a teenager because it was being taken over by those "dirty Ns and spics". I feel dirty just typing these words.

I don't think my parents were always so hateful. Before the riots they use to refer to African Americans as "colored people". They were something to be looked down upon, pitied, and my father generously contributed money to the "The United Negro College Fund". We even had an African American maid or ironing lady come to our house weekly to iron the clothes for our family of 9. That poor woman had to iron in our basement for 8 hours while us spoiled kids ran around upstairs calling each other Ns and "Jigaboos". I remember at one point her yelling to us upstairs to stop using those words. I think that was the first time I ever thought about how offensive those words were to her or any African American. I remember sitting next to her during lunch and watching her eat her sandwich and drink her tea. I remember staring at her facial features and observing her skin color and noticing how her palms where pink like mine. I also remember thinking why my mom hired her if she was such a bad person.

As I entered my teen years I remember rejecting my parents hateful mindset. During college I befriended a few African American women in my dorm. We would head over to colleges in PA to attend their Fraternity parties. I remember being shocked and hurt on one or two occasion as words were spoken inquiring what "they" were doing here. We were told which Frat house they would better enjoy. On the way home I was pulled over by State Troopers. I remember feeling my friends fear as the flashlights were set on them. This was 1980 for god's sake!

Anyway, the years have passed and I have fought like hell to erase the negative messages about race, religions, and sexual orientations. 10 years ago I was faced with the dilemma of wanting to expand my family through adoption. The wait for a white baby was years. The risk of FAS with adopting a white Russian baby was one I was not willing to take. My husband and I decided to adopt from South Korea after deciding that an African American baby would not be welcomed into my side of the family. My father even stated that Asian is a good choice of race because the are "superior" intelligence than our race. I am always vigilant to racist remarks from peers and happily have not had to intervene too often. Maybe there is hope for our youth?

Finally, I still have traces of prejudice. I am not totally without. A couple of weeks ago my car broke down on the way home from college. I stood outside in the cold 15 minutes before anyone stopped. Finally, one gentleman stopped and offered a ride to a gas station. He was African American. I am embarrassed to say that I hesitated for a few seconds. I had to look for other clues that he wasn't going to hurt me. I assessed his car and his clothing and his aura as friendly and professional before I took that ride. I wonder if I would have been so hesitant if he was white.

Moment of Silence

All: Jesus our friend and brother, through your life and your journey to the cross, your death and resurrection, you have shown us how to live in love. May we always follow your example, living in redemption, living a life of compassion, in the search for peace through justice for all your people.

Station 5: Jesus is Judged by Pilate

Leader: We adore you, oh Christ, and we bless you.
All: **Because by your holy cross you have redeemed the world.**

Reading:

The chief priests with the elders and the scribes, that is, the whole Sanhedrin, held a council. They bound Jesus, led him away, and handed him over to Pilate. Pilate questioned him, "Are you the king of the Jews?" He said to him in reply, "You say so." The chief priests accused him of many things. Again Pilate questioned him, "Have you no answer? See how many things they accuse you of." Jesus gave him no further answer, so that Pilate was amazed.... Pilate, wishing to satisfy the crowd, released Barrabas... [and] handed [Jesus] over to be crucified.
Mark 15: 1-5, 15

Moment of Silence

Story:

Illegal immigration and racism are problems that many countries face around the world. For example people from Haiti cross the border illegally to try to find work in the Dominican Republic and are victims of racism there. People from the Dominican Republic come illegally to Puerto Rico to find the jobs that Puerto Ricans don't want to do and they are subject to racism too. Puerto Ricans goes to the U.S. and they will be subject to the same.

If you have the opportunity to watch a soap opera from any Latin American country including Puerto Rico you will not find people of Indian or African descent not even mulatto's in starring roles they will only fill the roles of a driver, domestic service or poor people. What I trying to say with this is that we Latin Americans not only suffer from racism but we are racist too.

Racism is alive and well everywhere. United States is the most known and talk about case by being the most powerful nation in the world. Sadly the Nation has never been fully integrated. Some argue that the U.S. will lose its identity caused by wave after wave of legal and Illegal immigrants, others believe that the country is invaded as a part of a conspiracy by the Mexican government to take back what they lost in 1848. Now there is another conspiracy that the Mexicans were used as a part of a terrorist plot to destroy the U.S. with the Swine Flu and the list of conspiracies and hypothesis goes on and on.

What if those crossing the borders were Caucasians would they be subject to the same persecution? I think not. If the United States does not want to go down in flames, instead of segregate they must integrate those that come legally to the U.S. Some say the American culture will be lost but what is the American Culture if not a mix of different traditions brought by the very immigrants that came to the nation. Some say that English must be the official language of the nation because the immigrants speak other languages. That is right only in part the first generation will maintain it native tongue and traditions the second generation will mostly speak the language of the nation they are living in and begin to acquire its culture by the third they are only known perhaps by the color of the skin or their last names. That transition must be encouraged by integrating not segregating in ghettos by education and by our moral values. Aren't we all equal under the eyes of God?

Those who believe in racism have the rights too, we don't live in Nazi Germany. The United States value the Freedom of Speech and they have the right to believe and express whatever they think is correct.

The American People have two paths

1.   To leave racism and xenophobia behind and integrate the people who come legally into the U.S. and enrich the American Culture with their traditions.

2   Or fall into a Civil War that will destroy the Nation as we know it.

A final note we have to remember that we all came here as invaders in the late 15th century that we took their lands and destroyed innumerable cultures and commit genocide in a scale only compared with the Holocaust.

I wrote this after reading a news article about the backlash Mexicans are suffering due to Illegal immigration and the Swine Flu.

Moment of Silence

All: Jesus our friend and brother, through your life and your journey to the cross, your death and resurrection, you have shown us how to live in love. May we always follow your example, living in redemption, living a life of compassion, in the search for peace through justice for all your people.

Station 6: Jesus is Scourged and Crowned with Thorns

Leader: We adore you, oh Christ, and we bless you.
All: **Because by your holy cross you have redeemed the world.**

Reading:

Then Pilate took Jesus and had him scourged. And the soldiers wove a crown out of thorns and placed it on his head, and clothed him in a purple cloak, and they came to him and said,"Hail, King of the Jews!" And they struck him repeatedly.

John 19: 1-3

Moment of Silence

Story:

I was born and raised in Philadelphia in a mixed neighborhood, the word black or white never came up.

I moved to the dirty south and I can feel the difference when it comes to racism. Florida is 20 years behind the times!

I had a guy tell me he wants to secretly date me because his family don't believe in interracial dating. I had an 80 year old guy drive in his pickup truck in my neighborhood and yell "niggar town" over and over again.

I went to a job interview where I was the only black person in the building, I felt out of place and this is hardly heard of in Philadelphia.

It speaks for itself when you hear that the unemployment level for blacks is 18% and of whites 8%. We only make up 15% of the American population.

To be fair I heard a story of an American Israeli girl being called names because she is Jewish. I heard of stories of what American consider to be "Latino" discriminated against. So I know it's not just blacks.

Sometimes I feel like moving to a country where people look like me, but again I was raised in a mix neighborhood so I love to be around different races.

Moment of Silence

All: Jesus our friend and brother, through your life and your journey to the cross, your death and resurrection, you have shown us how to live in love. May we always follow your example, living in redemption, living a life of compassion, in the search for peace through justice for all your people.

Station 7: Jesus Bears the Cross

Leader: We adore you, oh Christ, and we bless you.
All: **Because by your holy cross you have redeemed the world.**

Reading:

When the chief priests and the guards saw [Jesus] they cried out, "Crucify him, crucify him!" Pilate said to them, "Take him yourselves and crucify him. I find no guilt in him." ... They cried out, "Take him away, take him away! Crucify him!" Pilate said to them, "Shall I crucify your king?" The chief priests answered, "We have no king but Caesar." Then he handed him over to them to be crucified. So they took Jesus, and carrying the cross himself he went out to what is called the Place of the Skull, in Hebrew,Golgotha.
John 19: 6, 15-17

Moment of Silence

Story:

A friend of mine forwarded a message about the white pride movement a few months ago, and I flipped out. I asked her why she felt she had to perpetuate divisions between people, to which she first tried to change the topic by saying she forgot I was Canadian (as if this was something she thought SHOULD be happening in the USA). Our conversation continued to little progress on the point; she thought it would have been something I was interested in, but couldn't articulate to me the answer to my first question.

Why is that so hard? The Black pride movement served its purpose to inspire an educationally disadvantaged people of the time to learn more and become great. I am nearly temped to say that such things should be a thing of the past, but I have seen too much of a similar attitude come from various places in society.

I've had friends turn cold when I responded this way, as if forming their little cliques about this idea will empower them. I've seen people change gears when there is nothing more about a person that is different but their skin or national origin. I've heard intolerance about a certain elected person because "we don't need a black man running this country".

These people lose me as a friend if they don't see the illogic in their statements after I point it out to them: People are not defined by their skin or nationality, but by their culture and experiences. I have abandoned a few friendships this way - I'll not support such rubbish, nor the people who believe it blindly.

Can you think without borders?

Moment of Silence

All: Jesus our friend and brother, through your life and your journey to the cross, your death and resurrection, you have shown us how to live in love. May we always follow your example, living in redemption, living a life of compassion, in the search for peace through justice for all your people.

Station 8: Jesus is Helped by Simon the Cyrenian to Carry the Cross

Leader: We adore you, oh Christ, and we bless you.
All: **Because by your holy cross you have redeemed the world.**

Reading:

 They pressed into service a passer-by, Simon, a Cyrenian, who was coming in from the country, the father of Alexander and Rufus, to carry his cross.
Mark 15: 21

Moment of Silence

Story:

First day of 2nd grade, and first day in a public school, I raced out of class and hopped on the bus full of excitement. I found an empty seat and plopped my 7 year old White boy self down next to the window and hoped someone I had met earlier rode my bus and would sit next to me.

I must have taken this kid's seat or something because a little black boy named Humphrey Holmes, came by, he must have been 9 or 10 years old by then, he saw me sitting there all happy and couldn't resist. He lifted me out of my seat, dropped me in the Aisle and said "Do it. I know you wanna call me a n****r!"

I had never heard the word before, I had no idea what it meant, but I understood he would possibly be hurt if I called him it, so I did..Racism wasn't an idea a 7 year old thinks up on his own, I didn't know, and haven't used it to hurt anyone since..

I spent two weeks in detention and got a 3 hour ride in the truck with my dad so he could explain racism to me. I honestly could have gone another year or two without that revelation. Humphrey racist paranoia spread more harm than good.

Needless to say I avoided interracial conversations for years after that, well you saw what happened the last time!

I'm way over that now and have many friends of all shapes and colors, but this was my first and only true racism experience.

Moment of Silence

All: Jesus our friend and brother, through your life and your journey to the cross, your death and resurrection, you have shown us how to live in love. May we always follow your example, living in redemption, living a life of compassion, in the search for peace through justice for all your people.

Station 9: Jesus Meets the Women of Jerusalem

Leader: We adore you, oh Christ, and we bless you.
All: **Because by your holy cross you have redeemed the world.**

Reading:

A large crowd of people followed Jesus, including many women who mourned and lamented him. Jesus turned to them and said, "Daughters of Jerusalem, do not weep for me; weep instead for yourselves and for your children, for indeed, the days are coming when people will say, 'Blessed are the barren, the wombs that never bore and the breasts that never nursed.' At that time, people will say to the mountains, 'Fall upon us!' and to the hills, 'Cover us!' for if these things are done when the wood is green what will happen when it is dry?"
Luke 23: 27-31

Moment of Silence

Story:

I was recently subjected to racism today, and I am so irritated and tired of all of it. It doesn't happen frequently, but when it does, it hurts me so much. This is my race they are talking about, this is who I AM. I haven't done anything to these people. ANYTHING. In fact I'm good to them, and they return the favor by being a bunch of ignorant pricks. You HAVE to be a narrow-minded fool to think that you are better than another person because of your race. It just doesn't make any sense why they would say this to me.

I was told today that my race is subordinate and degenerate, and a whole bunch of other things. The worst part about it all, is I didn't have a thing to say to this person. I wanted so bad to tell him off but I had no idea how. I didn't have the words to say anything back. It was not until later when I thought about this situation when I had the perfect response. It is so irritating!

They think they know so much about you but they don't. Most of these racist have no idea what it feels like to be felt lower than dirt. They live their whole lives without it, and they joke about it and have fun with it all the time, not taking into consideration the effect it has on other people.

I'm going to end this story with one simple question...
Why?

Moment of Silence

All: Jesus our friend and brother, through your life and your journey to the cross, your death and resurrection, you have shown us how to live in love. May we always follow your example, living in redemption, living a life of compassion, in the search for peace through justice for all your people.

Station 10: Jesus is Crucified

Leader: We adore you, oh Christ, and we bless you.
All: **Because by your holy cross you have redeemed the world.**

Reading:

When they came to the place called the Skull, they crucified him and the criminals there, one on his right, the other on his left. [Then Jesus said, "Father, forgive them, they know not what they do."]
Luke 23: 33-34

Moment of Silence

Story:

I   suppose I have a lot of reasons to hate people in general. I'm brown and have been discriminated against on several occasions (that's another story). However, I simply cannot find the evil inside of me that enjoys being cruel to nice/thoughtful people. I despise people who abuse children and animals. I hate stupid drivers that have no insurance. God saw fit to make me brown. He saw fit to bless others with their own unique color and culture as well. Who am I to question his knowledge?

Moment of Silence

All: Jesus our friend and brother, through your life and your journey to the cross, your death and resurrection, you have shown us how to live in love. May we always follow your example, living in redemption, living a life of compassion, in the search for peace through justice for all your people.

Station 11: Jesus Promises His Kingdom to the Good Thief

Leader: We adore you, oh Christ, and we bless you.
All: **Because by your holy cross you have redeemed the world.**

Reading:

Now one of the criminals hanging there reviled Jesus, saying, "Are you not the Messiah? Save yourself and us." The other, however, rebuking him, said in reply, "Have you no fear of God, for you are subject to the same condemnation? And indeed, we have been condemned justly, for the sentence we received corresponds to our crimes, but this man has done nothing criminal." Then he said, "Jesus, remember me when you come into your kingdom." He replied to him, "Amen, I say to you, today you will be with me in Paradise."
Luke 23: 39-43

Moment of Silence

Story:

I was waiting for a commuter rail to take me from Boston back to suburbs, with a number of drunken Red Sox fans. My people. One girl, who I read as white and about my age, had taken a broom from the janitor's closet and was using it to sweep the platform. Her friends and family appeared to be egging her on as she got up in waiting passengers' space to sweep by our feet. Eventually the janitor came to collect his broom, but she refused to give it back. In a turn of events that struck me as bizarre, two separate groups of people, one which appeared to be related to her and one that didn't, came to her defense, claiming that the broom was hers, when they knew otherwise. "She's doing a good job," they said," why don't you just let her sweep?"

That's where things started to get ugly. "I work for my money," she said, still sweeping. Then, loud enough for him to hear, "I take care of *my* kids", thus implying that he, a working class man of color, did not take care of his kids. In front of a platform of spectators she had stolen his supplies, refused to give them back and humiliated him. I can't explain how I know that this situation would not have been allowed to carry on for so long if she had not been white and he had not been a man of color, but I know that is why he could not simply take the broom back from her, but stood outside her circle of friends of family and patiently gestured that he needed his broom back. When his polite attempts failed, he went upstairs to get his boss, a white man, who came down and said little more than, "Jose needs his broom back," and then gently took it out of her hands, meeting little resistance from her or the crowd that had come to her defense.

On the train home, she started ranting about how that job should belong to an "American" anyway (as if she could have known whether he was a citizen or not,) and that the janitor should be deported. At this point, I moved to another car in the interest of her safety.

Moment of Silence

All: Jesus our friend and brother, through your life and your journey to the cross, your death and resurrection, you have shown us how to live in love. May we always follow your example, living in redemption, living a life of compassion, in the search for peace through justice for all your people.

Station 12: Jesus Speaks to His Mother and the Disciple

Leader: We adore you, oh Christ, and we bless you.
All: **Because by your holy cross you have redeemed the world.**

Reading:

Standing by the cross of Jesus were his mother and his mother's sister, Mary the wife of Clopas, and Mary of Magdala. When Jesus saw his mother and the disciple there whom he loved, he said to his mother, "Woman, behold, your son." Then he said to the disciple, "Behold, your mother." And from that hour the disciple took her into his home.
John 19: 25-27

Moment of Silence

Story:

When I was 16, one of my best friends was a white girl named Tasha. I never saw her parents. She went to public school, which was pretty rare because all the white people in our county sent their kids to private school while all the blacks went to the public school. Anyway, she really wanted me to come to her birthday party and sleepover. I told her I would come. When my mom dropped me off, I went into the house and I felt a thousand hateful eyes piercing into me. Her mom, who was really nice, spoke to me and told me to get some drinks out the fridge. I went to the fridge and I heard her stepfather say, "I don't want that gal touching my food." I told Tasha that I was leaving. She started to cry and begged me to stay. I felt horrible. It was a nightmare. Later that night, at the sleepover, I was the only black girl there. One of the other girls asked me, "Why does your hair look like that?" I remember telling her, "Why is your face so ugly?" They all started laughing. She told that she was sorry. That sleepover turned out ok.

Moment of Silence

All: Jesus our friend and brother, through your life and your journey to the cross, your death and resurrection, you have shown us how to live in love. May we always follow your example, living in redemption, living a life of compassion, in the search for peace through justice for all your people.

Station 13: Jesus Dies on the Cross

Leader: We adore you, oh Christ, and we bless you.
All: **Because by your holy cross you have redeemed the world.**

Reading:

It was now about noon and darkness came over the whole land until three in the afternoon because of an eclipse of the sun. Then the veil of the temple was torn down the middle. Jesus cried out in a loud voice, "Father, into your hands I commend my spirit"; and when he had said this he breathed his last. *Luke 23: 44-46*

Moment of Silence

Story:

When I was in 2nd grade, a white kid told me to go back to where I came from. Which is ridiculous, because I was born in the U.S. This experience has pretty much influenced my relationships with white people. The other experience that wasn't as blatant but was still kind of irritating was when my family got into a car accident. The fire department actually came by. All parties involved were brown people. Everyone started speaking at once, and one of the firemen put up his hand to shut us up and asked, "Do any of you speak English?" Which was kind of insulting, considering they were speaking in English, and not to mention the fact that both my parents are college -educated and have lived in this country for like 30 years. Interestingly, though, the most virulent racism I've witnessed has come from Asian Americans more than white people, which is kind of depressing.

Moment of Silence

All: Jesus our friend and brother, through your life and your journey to the cross, your death and resurrection, you have shown us how to live in love. May we always follow your example, living in redemption, living a life of compassion, in the search for peace through justice for all your people.

Station 14: Jesus is Placed in the Tomb

Leader: We adore you, oh Christ, and we bless you.
All: **Because by your holy cross you have redeemed the world.**

Reading:

When it was evening, there came a rich man from Arimathea named Joseph, who was himself a disciple of Jesus. He went to Pilate and asked for the body of Jesus; then Pilate ordered it to be handed over. Taking the body, Joseph wrapped it [in] clean linen and laid it in his new tomb that he had hewn in the rock. Then he rolled a huge stone across the entrance to the tomb and departed.
Matthew 27: 57-60

Moment of Silence

Story:

My Parents taught us life's lessons without ever even mentioning the words, black, white, race, prejudice etc.
I had friends - period, I played with anyone that was nice - period. Stayed away from bullies - period. I would never even once have thought of making fun of someone because of their race as I was taught to respect people unless they were bad and if they were , then I just stay away from them - period.

My Mother was a loving caring woman and everyone was welcome at our house, they taught us love and respect for man, animals and all nature. I try my best and think I have done pretty damn good to instill the same in my children.

As an adult I have lived my life the same way. I'm proud of that. AND I see now just how lucky I was!

Moment of Silence

All: Jesus our friend and brother, through your life and your journey to the cross, your death and resurrection, you have shown us how to live in love. May we always follow your example, living in redemption, living a life of compassion, in the search for peace through justice for all your people.

(The following should be read by a Youth if one is present and willing.)

Ladies and Gentlemen - I'm only going to talk to you just for a minute or so this evening. Because...

I have some very sad news for all of you, and I think sad news for all of our fellow citizens, and people who love peace all over the world, and that is that Martin Luther King was shot and was killed tonight in Memphis, Tennessee.

Martin Luther King dedicated his life to love and to justice between fellow human beings. He died in the cause of that effort. In this difficult day, in this difficult time for the United States, it's perhaps well to ask what kind of a nation we are and what direction we want to move in.

For those of you who are black - considering the evidence evidently is that there were white people who were responsible - you can be filled with bitterness, and with hatred, and a desire for revenge.

We can move in that direction as a country, in greater polarization - black people amongst blacks, and white amongst whites, filled with hatred toward one another. Or we can make an effort, as Martin Luther King did, to understand and to comprehend, and replace that violence, that stain of bloodshed that has spread across our land, with an effort to understand, compassion and love.

For those of you who are black and are tempted to be filled with hatred and mistrust of the injustice of such an act, against all white people, I would only say that I can also feel in my own heart the same kind of feeling. I had a member of my family killed, but he was killed by a white man.

But we have to make an effort in the United States, we have to make an effort to understand, to get beyond these rather difficult times.

My favorite poet was Aeschylus. He once wrote: "Even in our sleep, pain which cannot forget falls drop by drop upon the heart, until, in our own despair, against our will, comes wisdom through the awful grace of God."

What we need in the United States is not division; what we need in the United States is not hatred; what we need in the United States is not violence and lawlessness, but is love and wisdom, and compassion toward one another, and a feeling of justice toward those who still suffer within our country, whether they be white or whether they be black.

(Interrupted by applause)

So I ask you tonight to return home, to say a prayer for the family of Martin Luther King, yeah that's true, but more importantly to say a prayer for our own country, which all of us love - a prayer for understanding and that compassion of which I spoke. We can do well in this country. We will have difficult times. We've had difficult

121

times in the past. And we will have difficult times in the future. It is not the end of violence; it is not the end of lawlessness; and it's not the end of disorder.

But the vast majority of white people and the vast majority of black people in this country want to live together, want to improve the quality of our life, and want justice for all human beings that abide in our land.

(Interrupted by applause)

Let us dedicate ourselves to what the Greeks wrote so many years ago: to tame the savageness of man and make gentle the life of this world.

Let us dedicate ourselves to that, and say a prayer for our country and for our people. Thank you very much. (Applause)

Robert F. Kennedy - April 4, 1968

Just two months later, Robert Kennedy was gunned down during a celebration following his victory in the California primary, June 5, 1968.

Moment of Silence

"Darkness cannot drive out darkness,

only light can do that.

Hate cannot drive out hate;

only love can do that".

-Rev. Dr. Martin Luther King, Jr.

Leader:

Holy Trinity, we ask that you forgive us for the wrongs that we have done against each other. We thank you for bringing to this world such people as Rosa Parks, Rev. Dr. Martin Luther King, Jr. Caesar Chavez, Medgar Evers, Bobby Kennedy, Lyndon Johnson, Gandhi, Harriet Tubman, Sojourner Truth, Thurgood Marshal, Francisco Ramirez, Rev. Absalom Jones, John "Bud" Fowler, Paul Robeson, Rev. Richard Allen, Bp. James Theodore Holly, W.E.B. DuBois, Bp. Samuel David Ferguson, Rev. Pauli Murray, Jesse Owens, Eleanor Roosevelt and others who have worked and died for equality for all, and the saints no longer with us that we name now:

> (People are encouraged to say the names of other Saints that have **died** out loud)

and that we may follow in their example in Loving our neighbor as ourselves.

We thank you for those who have worked hard against Racism, Sexism, Homophobia, Classism, and for all of the other wrongs that we have done against each other. We also thank those who have taken the Anti-Racism training in this and other dioceses, and for those who give it.

Leader: Forgive us for remaining silent and bound by fear
All: Give us courage to speak and act with justice

Leader: Forgive us our arrogance in closing our eyes to other peoples and cultures
All: Forgive us for disfiguring this land and despoiling its bounty

Leader: Forgive us for despising the cultures of others, and taking away their self-respect
All: Give us grace to bind one another's wounds

Leader: Forgive us for not listening to the griefs of all who are oppressed in this land
All: Draw us together as one people

Leader: Forgive us for our prejudice and indifference towards those whose ways are different from our ways
All: Strengthen us to live with respect and compassion for one another

(All turn and fast each other in a circle if possible)

All:
I ask you my brothers and sisters in Christ, for forgiveness for the wrongs that I have done in the past towards you. From this time on, I will do my best to do no injustices towards all that I am with, and to be a shining example of the Love that the Holy Trinity has for us all.

Leader:
We are the body of Christ
All:
His spirit is with us

Leader:
May the Peace of the Lord be Always with you.
All:
And also with you.

(If this is being done in a church and/or a clergy person is present, Holy Communion <u>can</u> be held beginning here)

Leader:
 Go in Peace to love and serve the Lord
All:
 Thanks be to God.

Leader:
 As you leave, please greet each other in the Peace.

Sunset In The Bay Area by E.C. Williams, Jr.

Stations Of The Cross

Everyday Life Lessons

By Earl Clinton Williams, Jr.

Acclamations

What you are about to read and experience will hopefully make you think about the things that you do and how you can help to not only help the world to become a place where this subject will become a thing of the past, but it will hopefully help you into making better choices in the way that you treat others.

I would like to thank my parents, sister, nephews, aunts, uncles, cousins, the Quakers, The Episcopal Church, and those of other faiths who helped me to become the person that I am.

I would also like to give thanks to the Holy Trinity in guiding me through the process of putting this together. I only hope and pray that this is an instrument that will help this world become a better place.

I hope and pray that all of those that read and hear the stories to come will do an Act of Kindness to others, and when it is done to them that they Pass It Forward. Always remember YCMAD (You Can Make A Difference)

I would like to thank Lorielle New, an actress, artist and friend who made the picture that is on the front of these Stations. The title of the piece is "Madonna And Child" and is from her Icon Series. If you would be interested in seeing more of her wonderful work, and would be interested in buying a copy of her artwork, please visit www.loriellenew.com as she has it for sale. She has full copyright to the artwork, and it has been used here with her permission.

Station 1: Jesus in the Garden of Gethsemane

Leader: We adore you, oh Christ, and we bless you.
All: **Because by your holy cross you have redeemed the world.**

Reading:

Then Jesus came with them to a place called Gethsemane, and he said to his disciples, "Sit here while I go over there and pray." He took along Peter and the two sons of Zebedee, and began to feel sorrow and distress. Then he said to them, "My soul is sorrowful even to death. Remain here and keep watch with me." He advanced a little and fell prostrate in prayer, saying, "My Father, if it is possible, let this cup pass from me; yet, not as I will, but as you will." When he returned to his disciples he found them asleep. He said to Peter, "So you could not keep watch with me for one hour? Watch and pray that you may not undergo the test. The spirit is willing, but the flesh is weak."
Matthew 25:36-41

Moment of Silence

Leader: In the name of the Father

Every day is a new beginning. The mistakes from yesterday are now just lessons learned. Absorb the energy and possibility of today, acknowledge the simple beauty that can so easily be taken for granted, and look forward to another new beginning tomorrow.

Moment of Silence

Leader: In the name of the Son

It's not the people that stand by your side when you're at your best, but the ones who stand beside you when you're at your WORST that are your true friends.

Moment of Silence

Leader: In the name of the Holy Spirit

Tomorrow does not exist. Just in case you do not live to see tomorrow, make sure that your today was everything that you would ever want because that is exactly how your life will be left if tomorrow does not come for you. Remember, always go out with a bang and never leave loose ends untied. Use the good candles, go out to a fancy dinner, and kiss a stranger. You never know, you might only have one night left to really make it count.

All: Jesus our friend and brother, through your life and your journey to the cross, your death and resurrection, you have shown us how to live in love. May we always follow your example, living in redemption, living a life of compassion, in the search for peace through justice for all your people.

Station 2: Jesus, Betrayed by Judas, is Arrested

Leader: We adore you, oh Christ, and we bless you.

All: **Because by your holy cross you have redeemed the world.**

Reading:

 Then, while [Jesus] was still speaking, Judas, one of the Twelve, arrived, accompanied by a crowd with swords and clubs, who had come from the chief priests, the scribes, and the elders. His betrayer had arranged a signal with them, saying, "the man I shall kiss is the one; arrest him and lead him away securely." He came and immediately went over to him and said, "Rabbi." And he kissed him. At this they laid hands on him and arrested him.
Mark 14: 43-46

Moment of Silence

Leader: In the name of the Father

 Never cry for a person who purposely hurts you. Just smile and say, "Thank you for giving me a chance to find someone better than you."

Moment of Silence

Leader: In the name of the Son

 Stop thinking about the past, and don't worry too much about the future. Your presence at this moment is a precious gift. Stop thinking about what you don't have, what you wish you had, who walked out of your life, and whatever else that falls in that category. Think about what you have, who you have in your life, and how fortunate you are right now.

Moment of Silence

Leader: In the name of the Holy Spirit

 Isn't it funny how the people who know the least about you often have the most to say? Don't be one of these people, ever.

All: Jesus our friend and brother, through your life and your journey to the cross, your death and resurrection, you have shown us how to live in love. May we always follow your example, living in redemption, living a life of compassion, in the search for peace through justice for all your people.

Station 3: Jesus is Condemned by the Sanhedrin

Leader: We adore you, oh Christ, and we bless you.
All: **Because by your holy cross you have redeemed the world.**

Reading:

When day came the council of elders of the people met, both chief priests and scribes, and they brought him before their Sanhedrin. They said, "If you are the Messiah, tell us," but he replied to them, "If I tell you, you will not believe, and if I question, you will not respond. But from this time on the Son of Man will be seated at the right hand of the power of God." They all asked, "Are you then the Son of God?" He replied to them, "You say that I am." Then they said, "What further need have we for testimony? We have heard it from his own mouth."
Luke 22: 66-71

Moment of Silence

Leader: In the name of the Father
The hardships we go through in our lives teach us lessons for the betterment of the rest of our lives if we choose to learn from them. So let your past make you better, not bitter.

Moment of Silence

Leader: In the name of the Son
There comes a time when you have to stand up and shout: This is me darn it! I look the way I look, think the way I think, feel the way I feel, and love the way I love! I am whole, unique and complex. Take me or leave me! Stop trying to change me!

Moment Of Silence

Leader: In the name of the Holy Spirit
Don't fear failure so much that you refuse to try new things. The saddest summary of a life contains two descriptions: could have and should have.

All: Jesus our friend and brother, through your life and your journey to the cross, your death and resurrection, you have shown us how to live in love. May we always follow your example, living in redemption, living a life of compassion, in the search for peace through justice for all your people.

Station 4: Jesus is Denied by Peter

Leader: We adore you, oh Christ, and we bless you.
All: **Because by your holy cross you have redeemed the world.**

Reading:

Now Peter was sitting outside in the courtyard. One of the maids came over to him and said, "You too were with Jesus the Galilean." But he denied it in front of everyone, saying, "I do not know what you are talking about!" As he went out to the gate, another girl saw him and said to those who were there, "This man was with Jesus the Nazorean." Again he denied it with an oath, "I do not know the man!" A little later the bystanders came over and said to Peter, "Surely you too are one of them; even your speech gives you away." At that he began to curse and to swear, "I do not know the man." And immediately a cock crowed. Then Peter remembered the word that Jesus had spoken: "Before the cock crows you will deny me three times." He went out and began to weep bitterly.
Matthew 26: 69-75

Moment of Silence

Leader: In the name of the Father
Let bygones be bygones. Don't let old pain, old anger and the past consume you. Move on in life and live for today, not yesterday. Yes, sometimes it's hard to let go, sometimes it's hard to say goodbye, but sometimes it hurts a lot more to hang on. And no, we don't need to completely forget. We just need to recognize and accept what is already long gone.

Moment of Silence

Leader: In the name of the Son
Your mistakes should be your motivation, not your excuses.

Moment of Silence

Leader: In the name of the Holy Spirit
The adventure begins when we are born. The destination is death. So the journey is far superior to the destination. Make the journey worthwhile every single day, because the distance we each get to travel is a mystery.

All: Jesus our friend and brother, through your life and your journey to the cross, your death and resurrection, you have shown us how to live in love. May we always follow your example, living in redemption, living a life of compassion, in the search for peace through justice for all your people.

Station 5: Jesus is Judged by Pilate

Leader: We adore you, oh Christ, and we bless you.
All: **Because by your holy cross you have redeemed the world.**

Reading:

The chief priests with the elders and the scribes, that is, the whole Sanhedrin, held a council. They bound Jesus, led him away, and handed him over to Pilate. Pilate questioned him, "Are you the king of the Jews?" He said to him in reply, "You say so." The chief priests accused him of many things. Again Pilate questioned him, "Have you no answer? See how many things they accuse you of." Jesus gave him no further answer, so that Pilate was amazed.... Pilate, wishing to satisfy the crowd, released Barrabas... [and] handed [Jesus] over to be crucified.
Mark 15: 1-5, 15

Moment of Silence

Leader: In the name of the Father
True enough, many of us have been hurt, and are reluctant to trust someone to love us again. In order to avoid feelings of loneliness we must first learn to let go of our pasts, and try to embrace the fact that sometimes in life you will get hurt. Don't waste time building up walls, when you should be devoting your time to building bridges.

Moment of Silence

Leader: In the name of the Son
I've been walked on, used and forgotten and I don't regret one moment of it, because in those moments I've learned a lot. I've learned who I can trust and can't. I've learned the meaning of friendship. I've learned how to tell when people are lying and when they're sincere. I've learned how to be myself, and appreciate the truly great people in my life as they arrive.

Moment of Silence

Leader: In the name of the Holy Spirit
You can't change what has happened, but you can choose how you're going to deal with it. Only you can choose your mood, so stay positive and don't let negativity get you down.

All: Jesus our friend and brother, through your life and your journey to the cross, your death and resurrection, you have shown us how to live in love. May we always follow your example, living in redemption, living a life of compassion, in the search for peace through justice for all your people.

Station 6: Jesus is Scourged and Crowned with Thorns

Leader: We adore you, oh Christ, and we bless you.

All: **Because by your holy cross you have redeemed the world.**

Reading:

Then Pilate took Jesus and had him scourged. And the soldiers wove a crown out of thorns and placed it on his head, and clothed him in a purple cloak, and they came to him and said,"Hail, King of the Jews!" And they struck him repeatedly.
John 19: 1-3

Moment of Silence

Leader: In the name of the Father
Live life fully while you're here. Experience everything. Take care of yourself and your friends. Have fun, be crazy, be weird. Go out and screw up! You're going to anyway, so you might as well enjoy the process. Take the opportunity to learn from your mistakes: find the cause of your problem and eliminate it. Don't try to be perfect; just be an excellent example of being human.

Moment of Silence

Leader: In the name of the Son
You will always see what is wrong when you are doing it right. But you will rarely see what is right when you are comfortably in the routine of doing it wrong.

Moment of Silence

Leader: In the name of the Holy Spirit
Do not ask for fulfillment in all your life, but for patience to accept frustration. Do not ask for perfection in all you do, but for the wisdom to not repeat mistakes. Do not ask for more before saying, "Thank You" for what you have already received.

All: Jesus our friend and brother, through your life and your journey to the cross, your death and resurrection, you have shown us how to live in love. May we always follow your example, living in redemption, living a life of compassion, in the search for peace through justice for all your people.

Station 7: Jesus Bears the Cross

Leader: We adore you, oh Christ, and we bless you.
All: **Because by your holy cross you have redeemed the world.**

Reading:

When the chief priests and the guards saw [Jesus] they cried out, "Crucify him, crucify him!" Pilate said to them, "Take him yourselves and crucify him. I find no guilt in him." ... They cried out, "Take him away, take him away! Crucify him!" Pilate said to them, "Shall I crucify your king?" The chief priests answered, "We have no king but Caesar." Then he handed him over to them to be crucified. So they took Jesus, and carrying the cross himself he went out to what is called the Place of the Skull, in Hebrew,Golgotha.
John 19: 6, 15-17

Moment of Silence

Leader: In the name of the Father
When you say you'll meet someone at 11:00 AM, be there at 10:45. When you promise a check on the 30th, send it on the 28th. Whatever you agree to do, do it a bit more. Start with your family and friends, then extend it to everyone you deal with. News will soon get around that you are a person of your word.

Moment of Silence

Leader: In the name of the Son
A bar of iron costs $5, made into horseshoes its worth is $12, made into needles its worth is $3500, made into balance springs for watches, its worth is $300, 000. Your own value is determined also by what you are able to make of yourself.

Moment of Silence

Leader: In the name of the Holy Spirit
Don't rely on someone else for your happiness and self worth. Only you can be responsible for that. If you can't love and respect yourself – no one else will be able to make that happen. Accept who you are – completely; the good and the bad – and make changes as YOU see fit – not because you think someone else wants you to be different.

All: Jesus our friend and brother, through your life and your journey to the cross, your death and resurrection, you have shown us how to live in love. May we always follow your example, living in redemption, living a life of compassion, in the search for peace through justice for all your people.

Station 8: Jesus is Helped by Simon the Cyrenian to Carry the Cross

Leader: We adore you, oh Christ, and we bless you.
All: **Because by your holy cross you have redeemed the world.**

Reading:

They pressed into service a passer-by, Simon, a Cyrenian, who was coming in from the country, the father of Alexander and Rufus, to carry his cross.
Mark 15: 21

Moment of Silence

Leader: In the name of the Father
When we continue to let someone in our lives repeatedly hurt us, we are saying to them that they matter more to us than our self-respect and our dignity. In order to take a stand for ourselves we must be willing to part ways with people whom we know that we've given a significant amount of chances to. Though letting go can sometimes cause us a lot of pain, it's necessary for us to provide the best future possible for ourselves.

Moment of Silence

Leader: In the name of the Son
It is better to wait for years for that someone you are sure of, than to continually grab a chance with someone who picks you up, but drops you whenever they want to.

Moment of Silence

Leader: In the name of the Holy Spirit
Often people attempt to live their lives backwards. They try to acquire more things, or more money, in order to do more of what they want, so they will be happier. The way it actually works is the reverse. You must first be who you really are, then do what you need to do, in order to have what you want.

All: Jesus our friend and brother, through your life and your journey to the cross, your death and resurrection, you have shown us how to live in love. May we always follow your example, living in redemption, living a life of compassion, in the search for peace through justice for all your people.

Station 9: Jesus Meets the Women of Jerusalem

Leader: We adore you, oh Christ, and we bless you.
All: **Because by your holy cross you have redeemed the world.**

Reading:

A large crowd of people followed Jesus, including many women who mourned and lamented him. Jesus turned to them and said, "Daughters of Jerusalem, do not weep for me; weep instead for yourselves and for your children, for indeed, the days are coming when people will say, 'Blessed are the barren, the wombs that never bore and the breasts that never nursed.' At that time, people will say to the mountains, 'Fall upon us!' and to the hills, 'Cover us!' for if these things are done when the wood is green what will happen when it is dry?"
Luke 23: 27-31

Moment of Silence

Leader: In the name of the Father
Respect isn't something you get by saying all the right words. Words can easily be a lie to get what you want. Respect is an attitude of acknowledging the feelings of another. You get respect for how you act and how you treat other people.

Moment of Silence

Leader: In the name of the Son
Do not become possessive. The purpose of a relationship is to complement each other, grow together, and achieve your common goals as a couple. At the same time, you must each maintain your individual identity as a human being.

Moment of Silence

Leader: In the name of the Holy Spirit
Don't live in the past, thinking about mistakes or changes you made. Think of your life as a book, move forward, close one chapter and open another. Learn from your mistakes, but focus on your future, not on your past.

All: Jesus our friend and brother, through your life and your journey to the cross, your death and resurrection, you have shown us how to live in love. May we always follow your example, living in redemption, living a life of compassion, in the search for peace through justice for all your people.

Station 10: Jesus is Crucified

Leader: We adore you, oh Christ, and we bless you.
All: **Because by your holy cross you have redeemed the world.**

Reading:

When they came to the place called the Skull, they crucified him and the criminals there, one on his right, the other on his left. [Then Jesus said, "Father, forgive them, they know not what they do."] *Luke 23: 33-34*

Moment of Silence

Leader: In the name of the Father
Happiness comes when we stop complaining about the troubles we have and offer thanks for all the troubles we don't have. Every day take the time to find something that makes your heart laugh and your soul smile. We all face difficult times in our lives, but do not let your circumstances weigh you down. Happiness is a choice... choose to be happy, and you will be.

Moment of Silence

Leader: In the name of the Son
We often want everything to stay the same, but feelings fade and people change. There are people who we think will be in our lives forever that become distant memories of our past. Do not fret. Feelings fading, and people changing is a part of life, and if you are growing as a person, not everyone will grow with you. You don't have to forget your past, instead learn from it and use this wisdom to choose the people who will surround you in the future.

Moment of Silence

Leader: In the name of the Holy Spirit
Just because life throws change at you, doesn't necessarily mean that a negative outcome is on the way horizon, it just means that life is happening as it naturally does, in seasons. Many of us tend to avoid change because we feel that we lose a sense of control and stability that we had in our lives before. Changes may happen in your life may seem overwhelming, but TRUST in yourself and know that there is nothing that life throws at you that you can't handle.

All: Jesus our friend and brother, through your life and your journey to the cross, your death and resurrection, you have shown us how to live in love. May we always follow your example, living in redemption, living a life of compassion, in the search for peace through justice for all your people.

Station 11: Jesus Promises His Kingdom to the Good Thief

Leader: We adore you, oh Christ, and we bless you.
All: **Because by your holy cross you have redeemed the world.**

Reading:

Now one of the criminals hanging there reviled Jesus, saying, "Are you not the Messiah? Save yourself and us." The other, however, rebuking him, said in reply, "Have you no fear of God, for you are subject to the same condemnation? And indeed, we have been condemned justly, for the sentence we received corresponds to our crimes, but this man has done nothing criminal." Then he said, "Jesus, remember me when you come into your kingdom." He replied to him, "Amen, I say to you, today you will be with me in Paradise."
Luke 23: 39-43

Moment of Silence

Leader: In the name of the Father
We have all been through situations and dealt with people we really care about who can sometimes make us feel insignificant. Never let your circumstances make you feel less than who you are. You know what you are capable of. Remind yourself that even in the midst of dark times, great things are in the horizon.

Moment of Silence

Leader: In the name of the Son
One day at a time – this is enough. Do not look back and grieve over the past for it is gone. And do not be troubled about the future, for it has yet to come. Live in the present, tomorrow is never promised, so make it so beautiful it will be worth remembering. Happiness is a journey, just as life is. Enjoy the ride.

Moment of Silence

Leader: In the name of the Holy Spirit
"I'm letting go of negative feelings, people, memories and thoughts in my life. I have no room for them and will only think positive and happy thoughts from now on." – Say this every morning, then practice. It will make a difference in your life, guaranteed.

All: Jesus our friend and brother, through your life and your journey to the cross, your death and resurrection, you have shown us how to live in love. May we always follow your example, living in redemption, living a life of compassion, in the search for peace through justice for all your people.

Station 12: Jesus Speaks to His Mother and the Disciple

Leader: We adore you, oh Christ, and we bless you.
All: **Because by your holy cross you have redeemed the world.**

Reading:

Standing by the cross of Jesus were his mother and his mother's sister, Mary the wife of Clopas, and Mary of Magdala. When Jesus saw his mother and the disciple there whom he loved, he said to his mother, "Woman, behold, your son." Then he said to the disciple, "Behold, your mother." And from that hour the disciple took her into his home.
John 19: 25-27

Moment of Silence

Leader: In the name of the Father
Don't wait until it's too late to tell someone how much you love and care for them, because when they're gone, no matter how loud you shout and cry, they won't be able to hear you anymore. And don't make someone keep waiting , even if you know they will. Eventually they will be forced to stop, and you will be back to wanting what you can't have.

Moment of Silence

Leader: In the name of the Son
Some people spend half of their lives complaining about the shortness of life's span and the other half killing time. Learn to make the most of life. Lose not a single day – time can never bring back what was swept away. Live life with a joyful heart and keep your spirit free and young. Enjoy the journey.

Moment of Silence

Leader: In the name of the Holy Spirit
Life is short, don't waste time worrying about what people think of you. As the saying goes... "Be more concerned with your character than your reputation, because your character is what you really are, while your reputation is what others think you are."

All: Jesus our friend and brother, through your life and your journey to the cross, your death and resurrection, you have shown us how to live in love. May we always follow your example, living in redemption, living a life of compassion, in the search for peace through justice for all your people.

Station 13: Jesus Dies on the Cross

Leader: We adore you, oh Christ, and we bless you.
All: **Because by your holy cross you have redeemed the world.**

Reading:

It was now about noon and darkness came over the whole land until three in the afternoon because of an eclipse of the sun. Then the veil of the temple was torn down the middle. Jesus cried out in a loud voice, "Father, into your hands I commend my spirit"; and when he had said this he breathed his last. *Luke 23: 44-46*

Moment of Silence

Leader: In the name of the Father
When those around you are inspired, they will inspire you. When those around you are positive, they will positively shift you. When those around you smile at you, it auto-encourages a smile back from you. When others are respectful of you, it creates appreciation and confidence in you. If you need extra positivity make it a priority to actively seek and befriend positive people.

Moment of Silence

Leader: In the name of the Son
Do all the good you can, by all the means you can, in all the ways you can, in all the places you can, at all the times you can, to all the people you can, for as long as you can.

Moment of Silence

Leader: In the name of the Holy Spirit
Life's curve-balls are thrown for a reason - to shift your path into a direction that is meant for you. You may not see or understand everything the moment it happens. And it may be tough. But reflect back on those negative curve-balls thrown at you in the past. You'll often see that eventually they lead you to a better place, person, state of mind, or situation.

All: Jesus our friend and brother, through your life and your journey to the cross, your death and resurrection, you have shown us how to live in love. May we always follow your example, living in redemption, living a life of compassion, in the search for peace through justice for all your people.

Station 14: Jesus is Placed in the Tomb

Leader: We adore you, oh Christ, and we bless you.
All: **Because by your holy cross you have redeemed the world.**

Reading:

When it was evening, there came a rich man from Arimathea named Joseph, who was himself a disciple of Jesus. He went to Pilate and asked for the body of Jesus; then Pilate ordered it to be handed over. Taking the body, Joseph wrapped it [in] clean linen and laid it in his new tomb that he had hewn in the rock. Then he rolled a huge stone across the entrance to the tomb and departed.
Matthew 27: 57-60

Moment of Silence

Leader: In the name of the Father
As you strive to achieve your goals and dreams you can count on there being some fairly substantial disappointments along the way. Don't get discouraged, the road to your dreams may not be an easy one. Think of these disappointments as challenges – tests of persistence and courage – that life throws at you during your journey. They are necessary and are meant to help you grow as a person.

Moment of Silence

Leader: In the name of the Son
Be vulnerable. Allow yourself to feel, to be open and authentic. Tear down any emotional brick walls you have built around yourself and feel every exquisite emotion, both good and bad. This is real life. This is how you welcome new opportunities.

Moment of Silence

Leader: In the name of the Holy Spirit
Everyone wants a perfect ending. But over the years I've learned that some of the best poems don't rhyme, and many great stories don't have a clear beginning, middle, or end. Life is about not knowing, embracing change, and taking a moment and making the best of it without knowing what's going to happen next.

All: Jesus our friend and brother, through your life and your journey to the cross, your death and resurrection, you have shown us how to live in love. May we always follow your example, living in redemption, living a life of compassion, in the search for peace through justice for all your people.

Artwork By Jananie Pryiaa

143

Stations Of The Cross

sorry.

I'm Sorry And I Apologize

By Earl Clinton Williams, Jr.

Acclamations

What you are about to read and listen to is about Apologizing. Do you avoid apologizing to others? when you have done wrong? Do others apologize to you when they have done wrong? Reflect upon what you are about to experience.

I would like to thank my parents, my sister, my nephews, my relatives, friends, the Episcopal Church, and the Quakers, along with many others who helped me become the person that I am.

I would also like to give thanks to the Holy Trinity in guiding me through the process of putting this together. I only hope and pray that this is an instrument that will help this world become a better place.

Station 1: Jesus in the Garden of Gethsemane

-

Leader: We adore you, oh Christ, and we bless you.
All: **Because by your holy cross you have redeemed the world.**

Reading:

Then Jesus came with them to a place called Gethsemane, and he said to his disciples, "Sit here while I go over there and pray." He took along Peter and the two sons of Zebedee, and began to feel sorrow and distress. Then he said to them, "My soul is sorrowful even to death. Remain here and keep watch with me." He advanced a little and fell prostrate in prayer, saying, "My Father, if it is possible, let this cup pass from me; yet, not as I will, but as you will." When he returned to his disciples he found them asleep. He said to Peter, "So you could not keep watch with me for one hour? Watch and pray that you may not undergo the test. The spirit is willing, but the flesh is weak."
Matthew 25:36-41

Moment of Silence

Story:

When I have wronged others, I humble myself and admit it. It strengthens bonds and cements friendships. Unless the wrong has crushed and destroyed. Sometimes it's difficult for us to do, but that is because pride is ruling as king. It takes strength and chutzpah to admit when we are wrong. But it makes us free and happy that we have. We all make mistakes and not one of us doesn't. On the other hand. when someone commits a mistake that affects us, then we should show mercy and forgive them, too. Especially when they are sorry for doing it. We are in this thing together.

Moment of Silence

All: Living, loving Spirit, let me practice forgiveness today by starting with the little hurts. I will let go of all the everyday occurrences that do not go the way I want, and the moment I begin to feel the familiar feeling of anger or resentment, I will practice forgiveness by invoking your loving and peaceful Presence and allowing divine grace to surround me. And so it is..

Station 2: Jesus, Betrayed by Judas, is Arrested

Leader: We adore you, oh Christ, and we bless you.
All: **Because by your holy cross you have redeemed the world.**

Reading:

Then, while [Jesus] was still speaking, Judas, one of the Twelve, arrived, accompanied by a crowd with swords and clubs, who had come from the chief priests, the scribes, and the elders. His betrayer had arranged a signal with them, saying, "the man I shall kiss is the one; arrest him and lead him away securely." He came and immediately went over to him and said, "Rabbi." And he kissed him. At this they laid hands on him and arrested him.
Mark 14: 43-46

Moment of Silence

Story:

When we have wronged someone, it is always the right thing to do and apologize. It makes for better relationships and a clean conscience. I have never had a problem doing that. My conscience doesn't allow me to know that I have offended or hurt someone and not apologize. Sometimes even after they have accepted my apology, I will feel really bad and beat myself up with it. I have since learned what not to do to cause these apologies to have to happen. And I'm going to be more cognizant of this in the future.

Moment of Silence

All: Living, loving Spirit, let me practice forgiveness today by starting with the little hurts. I will let go of all the everyday occurrences that do not go the way I want, and the moment I begin to feel the familiar feeling of anger or resentment, I will practice forgiveness by invoking your loving and peaceful Presence and allowing divine grace to surround me. And so it is.

Station 3: Jesus is Condemned by the Sanhedrin

Leader: We adore you, oh Christ, and we bless you.
All: **Because by your holy cross you have redeemed the world.**

Reading:

When day came the council of elders of the people met, both chief priests and scribes, and they brought him before their Sanhedrin. They said, "If you are the Messiah, tell us," but he replied to them, "If I tell you, you will not believe, and if I question, you will not respond. But from this time on the Son of Man will be seated at the right hand of the power of God." They all asked, "Are you then the Son of God?" He replied to them, "You say that I am." Then they said, "What further need have we for testimony? We have heard it from his own mouth."
Luke 22: 66-71

Moment of Silence

Story:

I am not too big, too arrogant or ignorant to say Sorry when I have wronged you As you mature, grow and find out who you are as a person, you also realize how important the word 'Sorry' is - its sadly over used, and under appreciated....

But when used correctly, with the right sincerity and emotion and contrition, then apologies and the word mean the right thing to the wronged person....

Moment of Silence

All: Living, loving Spirit, let me practice forgiveness today by starting with the little hurts. I will let go of all the everyday occurrences that do not go the way I want, and the moment I begin to feel the familiar feeling of anger or resentment, I will practice forgiveness by invoking your loving and peaceful Presence and allowing divine grace to surround me. And so it is..

Station 4: Jesus is Denied by Peter

Leader: We adore you, oh Christ, and we bless you.
All: **Because by your holy cross you have redeemed the world.**

Reading:

Now Peter was sitting outside in the courtyard. One of the maids came over to him and said, "You too were with Jesus the Galilean." But he denied it in front of everyone, saying, "I do not know what you are talking about!" As he went out to the gate, another girl saw him and said to those who were there, "This man was with Jesus the Nazorean." Again he denied it with an oath, "I do not know the man!" A little later the bystanders came over and said to Peter, "Surely you too are one of them; even your speech gives you away." At that he began to curse and to swear, "I do not know the man." And immediately a cock crowed. Then Peter remembered the word that Jesus had spoken: "Before the cock crows you will deny me three times." He went out and began to weep bitterly.
Matthew 26: 69-75

Moment of Silence

Story:

I used to have trouble with this and mainly it was a pride thing, with a little 'don't want to appear weak' sprinkled in. But as I got older I realized that being wrong or 'wronging someone' is usually only a big deal if you don't own up. I have always admired honest people and one of the characteristics of an honest person in my experience has been that they do apologize when they have wronged.

The surprising thing for me was how good it made me feel when I began to do this; it almost felt like a weight had been lifted from my shoulders. I never realized how small it made me feel to not come forward and apologize.

Moment of Silence

All: Living, loving Spirit, let me practice forgiveness today by starting with the little hurts. I will let go of all the everyday occurrences that do not go the way I want, and the moment I begin to feel the familiar feeling of anger or resentment, I will practice forgiveness by invoking your loving and peaceful Presence and allowing divine grace to surround me. And so it is..

Station 5: Jesus is Judged by Pilate

Leader: We adore you, oh Christ, and we bless you.
All: **Because by your holy cross you have redeemed the world.**

Reading:

The chief priests with the elders and the scribes, that is, the whole Sanhedrin, held a council. They bound Jesus, led him away, and handed him over to Pilate. Pilate questioned him, "Are you the king of the Jews?" He said to him in reply, "You say so." The chief priests accused him of many things. Again Pilate questioned him, "Have you no answer? See how many things they accuse you of." Jesus gave him no further answer, so that Pilate was amazed.... Pilate, wishing to satisfy the crowd, released Barrabas... [and] handed [Jesus] over to be crucified.
Mark 15: 1-5, 15

Moment of Silence

Story:

I am more than willing to say "I'm Sorry" when I have wronged someone or done something wrong. It's not a big deal to me being honest, I would much rather apologize than let things simmer or get worse. It's not that I say it without meaning it, if I say it I mean it, it's just that if I am in the wrong I have no difficulty putting my hands up and admitting.

True, it's not always straight away but even if it's a day or so later I will try and speak to someone and apologize. Better than that I am becoming more aware of what I am saying and doing and now find I do not feel the need to apologize quite as much.

If you are wrong I really don't see the problem in putting up your hands and admitting to it.

Moment of Silence

All: Living, loving Spirit, let me practice forgiveness today by starting with the little hurts. I will let go of all the everyday occurrences that do not go the way I want, and the moment I begin to feel the familiar feeling of anger or resentment, I will practice forgiveness by invoking your loving and peaceful Presence and allowing divine grace to surround me. And so it is..

Station 6: Jesus is Scourged and Crowned with Thorns

Leader: We adore you, oh Christ, and we bless you.

All: **Because by your holy cross you have redeemed the world.**

Reading:

 Then Pilate took Jesus and had him scourged. And the soldiers wove a crown out of thorns and placed it on his head, and clothed him in a purple cloak, and they came to him and said,"Hail, King of the Jews!" And they struck him repeatedly.

John 19: 1-3

Moment of Silence

 I'm a stubborn, hard headed person. Yes, I admit it. My mind enjoys thinking that it's right all the time and if you want to tangle yourself in a debate with me, I'll likely make you wish you hadn't. I don't "fight" to be right. I simply presume that I usually am.

However..

People are more important than my need to be right.. and as a person who is continually evolving, changing, [and hopefully] growing into a better "me", I am learning more and more that in order to be a healthy self, I need to be willing to not only admit that I have hurt or wronged another person, but be willing to do what it takes to make amends.

Even the most introverted of individuals needs human contact in order to thrive. We often get so entangled in our own feelings of being wronged that we become blind to our ability to harm the feelings of those around us. But even while we think we're hurting no one with our constant propensity to focus only on ourselves, we are doing unseen damage. Selfishness and self-absorption does do harm. It does inflict invisible wounds. And it does require time and tenderness to heal those wounds.. but first, we have to acknowledge our wrongdoing and make up our minds to leave it behind us for the betterment of someone else.

If I have to choose between being "right" or being the "victim" and being willing to put my pride away long enough to care about the feelings of someone else, I would rather do the latter.

No matter how awesome you think you are, there is always room for improvement.

When in doubt, I choose to apologize -- and I choose to forgive.

Moment of Silence

All: Living, loving Spirit, let me practice forgiveness today by starting with the little hurts. I will let go of all the everyday occurrences that do not go the way I want, and the moment I begin to feel the familiar feeling of anger or resentment, I will practice forgiveness by invoking your loving and peaceful Presence and allowing divine grace to surround me. And so it is..

Station 7: Jesus Bears the Cross

Leader: We adore you, oh Christ, and we bless you.
All: **Because by your holy cross you have redeemed the world.**

Reading:

When the chief priests and the guards saw [Jesus] they cried out, "Crucify him, crucify him!" Pilate said to them, "Take him yourselves and crucify him. I find no guilt in him." ... They cried out, "Take him away, take him away! Crucify him!" Pilate said to them, "Shall I crucify your king?" The chief priests answered, "We have no king but Caesar." Then he handed him over to them to be crucified. So they took Jesus, and carrying the cross himself he went out to what is called the Place of the Skull, in Hebrew, Golgotha.
John 19: 6, 15-17

Moment of Silence

Story:

Don't we all screw up sometimes? Don't we all cause pain to someone at some point? Well, I do –sometimes. It's painful to me as well. The discomfort of having wronged someone can haunt me. That's why I just need to apologize when I realize I've done so. And that's also why I avoid behaviors where I'll have to apologize.

This is how:

I don't talk when I'm angry. This may be difficult at times when the other person presses my hot-buttons. But I still try to zip it and act cool even though I may be boiling inside. So I don't say nasty things to people.

I don't do things that I will be ashamed of. I don't make promises I can't keep. I know sometimes people expect me to promise them something but I won't promise anything just to be nice. I don't cheat, I don't deceive people.

My pitfalls:

Impatience. This can result to wrongly judge someone too soon. Also, I want results –soon- so I often patronize people and I make them feel like they're inadequate, not good enough. Sarcasm. I might hurt someone's feelings without knowing.

Unfortunately, saying "I'm sorry" isn't always enough; it doesn't make people feel any better; it doesn't undo the wrong. People don't mind the reasons why I did it. They mind *the fact* that I did it.
Acknowledging my mistake and asking for their forgiveness is the first thing I do. I always try to be honest and truthful and I don't come up with poor excuses for myself. I also ask them how I can make it right. This last bit is tricky because not always can I respond to their request and then I feel parting is the best for both parties.

Moment of Silence

All: Living, loving Spirit, let me practice forgiveness today by starting with the little hurts. I will let go of all the everyday occurrences that do not go the way I want, and the moment I begin to feel the familiar feeling of anger or resentment, I will practice forgiveness by invoking your loving and peaceful Presence and allowing divine grace to surround me. And so it is.

Station 8: Jesus is Helped by Simon the Cyrenian to Carry the Cross

Leader: We adore you, oh Christ, and we bless you.
All: **Because by your holy cross you have redeemed the world.**

Reading:

They pressed into service a passer-by, Simon, a Cyrenian, who was coming in from the country, the father of Alexander and Rufus, to carry his cross.
Mark 15: 21

Moment of Silence

Story:

I've made it into a sort of motto for myself. Never apologize for speaking your mind and always apologize when you're wrong.

It's a tough motto to stick to but I try hard.

There's nothing shameful about apologizing. In fact, it's the fair, ethical thing to do. I would expect it from others, so why should the standards be any less stringent for my own self?

A big personal benefit of apologizing when you're wrong is that it puts me into a much more receptive mindset. It gives me a chance to improve, to learn, instead of forcing me to blunder on with all sorts of illusions, clinging to them steadfastly despite objections. It keeps me grounded. We're all fallible. I feel no shame in admitting my fallibility - at least I'm honest about it.

In practice though, there are always barriers to apologizing. Social norms play a part. It's a blow to the ego (most people ARE egotistical to some extent). It doesn't feel good to admit you're wrong. But in the long run, it's the best policy and I always strive to get rid of the momentary impulses of vanity and pride. Being honest has it's benefits.

Moment of Silence

All: Living, loving Spirit, let me practice forgiveness today by starting with the little hurts. I will let go of all the everyday occurrences that do not go the way I want, and the moment I begin to feel the familiar feeling of anger or resentment, I will practice forgiveness by invoking your loving and peaceful Presence and allowing divine grace to surround me. And so it is.

Station 9: Jesus Meets the Women of Jerusalem

Leader: We adore you, oh Christ, and we bless you.
All: **Because by your holy cross you have redeemed the world.**

Reading:

A large crowd of people followed Jesus, including many women who mourned and lamented him. Jesus turned to them and said, "Daughters of Jerusalem, do not weep for me; weep instead for yourselves and for your children, for indeed, the days are coming when people will say, 'Blessed are the barren, the wombs that never bore and the breasts that never nursed.' At that time, people will say to the mountains, 'Fall upon us!' and to the hills, 'Cover us!' for if these things are done when the wood is green what will happen when it is dry?"
Luke 23: 27-31

Moment of Silence

Story:

To acknowledge you're wrong takes courage and strength and to me it is a sign of greatness and respect. We could easily say nothing in some cases or allow for time to be the great healer.

When a person openly apologizes with sincerity it touches you deeply, yet some shy away from this hoping you'd forget or let it pass for some sorry is the hardest word.

Some feel uncomfortable and would rather skip over that unpleasant moment, yet it takes a man of integrity and value and character to show his true worth.

Moment of Silence

All: Living, loving Spirit, let me practice forgiveness today by starting with the little hurts. I will let go of all the everyday occurrences that do not go the way I want, and the moment I begin to feel the familiar feeling of anger or resentment, I will practice forgiveness by invoking your loving and peaceful Presence and allowing divine grace to surround me. And so it is..

Station 10: Jesus is Crucified

Leader: We adore you, oh Christ, and we bless you.
All: **Because by your holy cross you have redeemed the world.**

Reading:

When they came to the place called the Skull, they crucified him and the criminals there, one on his right, the other on his left. [Then Jesus said, "Father, forgive them, they know not what they do."]
Luke 23: 33-34

Moment of Silence

Story:

I think its wrong to NOT apologize when you have done something wrong. I think its important for everyone to take responsibility for their actions and if they don't, then they're just weak. I know that may be harsh, but its true and you just have to deal wit it because that's part of life, taking responsibility for what you did.

Moment of Silence

All: Living, loving Spirit, let me practice forgiveness today by starting with the little hurts. I will let go of all the everyday occurrences that do not go the way I want, and the moment I begin to feel the familiar feeling of anger or resentment, I will practice forgiveness by invoking your loving and peaceful Presence and allowing divine grace to surround me. And so it is..

Station 11: Jesus Promises His Kingdom to the Good Thief

Leader: We adore you, oh Christ, and we bless you.

All: **Because by your holy cross you have redeemed the world.**

Reading:

Now one of the criminals hanging there reviled Jesus, saying, "Are you not the Messiah? Save yourself and us." The other, however, rebuking him, said in reply, "Have you no fear of God, for you are subject to the same condemnation? And indeed, we have been condemned justly, for the sentence we received corresponds to our crimes, but this man has done nothing criminal." Then he said, "Jesus, remember me when you come into your kingdom." He replied to him, "Amen, I say to you, today you will be with me in Paradise."
Luke 23: 39-43

Moment of Silence

Story:

I'm not too proud to admit I screwed up. It's usually the quickest way to fix things. Even when it doesn't fix things, at least I've done all I can. I learned the value of apologizing when I worked for this awesome hard-nosed German lady. When I did something stupid, it was no use trying to explain. She would say, "No excuses, just fix it!" So I learned to just admit it as soon as I realized it, apologize, and get to working fixing it. The same thing seems to work in relationships. No excuses!

Moment of Silence

All: Living, loving Spirit, let me practice forgiveness today by starting with the little hurts. I will let go of all the everyday occurrences that do not go the way I want, and the moment I begin to feel the familiar feeling of anger or resentment, I will practice forgiveness by invoking your loving and peaceful Presence and allowing divine grace to surround me. And so it is..

Station 12: Jesus Speaks to His Mother and the Disciple

Leader: We adore you, oh Christ, and we bless you.
All: **Because by your holy cross you have redeemed the world.**

Reading:

Standing by the cross of Jesus were his mother and his mother's sister, Mary the wife of Clopas, and Mary of Magdala. When Jesus saw his mother and the disciple there whom he loved, he said to his mother, "Woman, behold, your son." Then he said to the disciple, "Behold, your mother." And from that hour the disciple took her into his home.
John 19: 25-27

Moment of Silence

Story:

Usually an apology initiates the forgiveness process. Some people can forgive without receiving an apology, but those people are rare in my experience. When someone truly forgives, they let go of the hurt and anger they feel.

If I have wronged someone, I have hurt them once. To not apologize delays that forgiveness and extends the hurt that they feel. This wrongs them a second time.

Also, offering an apology can help build stronger relationships. You thought enough of the other person to apologize to them. They see that.

There is no shame in apologizing.

Moment of Silence

All: Living, loving Spirit, let me practice forgiveness today by starting with the little hurts. I will let go of all the everyday occurrences that do not go the way I want, and the moment I begin to feel the familiar feeling of anger or resentment, I will practice forgiveness by invoking your loving and peaceful Presence and allowing divine grace to surround me. And so it is..

Station 13: Jesus Dies on the Cross

Leader: We adore you, oh Christ, and we bless you.
All: **Because by your holy cross you have redeemed the world.**

Reading:

It was now about noon and darkness came over the whole land until three in the afternoon because of an eclipse of the sun. Then the veil of the temple was torn down the middle. Jesus cried out in a loud voice, "Father, into your hands I commend my spirit"; and when he had said this he breathed his last. *Luke 23: 44-46*

Moment of Silence

Story:

I think I've proven it. I know when I've crossed the limit and hurt someone and though not intentional, sometime the mouth (or fingers) start running before the brain can jump in. I don't do it just to do it though, I must be provoked, and then it starts. If I'm in the wrong I do apologize. Even if the other person doesn't or refuses to admit that they too are guilty, at least I've made my peace.

Moment of Silence

All: Living, loving Spirit, let me practice forgiveness today by starting with the little hurts. I will let go of all the everyday occurrences that do not go the way I want, and the moment I begin to feel the familiar feeling of anger or resentment, I will practice forgiveness by invoking your loving and peaceful Presence and allowing divine grace to surround me. And so it is.

Station 14: Jesus is Placed in the Tomb

Leader: We adore you, oh Christ, and we bless you.
All: **Because by your holy cross you have redeemed the world.**

Reading:

When it was evening, there came a rich man from Arimathea named Joseph, who was himself a disciple of Jesus. He went to Pilate and asked for the body of Jesus; then Pilate ordered it to be handed over. Taking the body, Joseph wrapped it [in] clean linen and laid it in his new tomb that he had hewn in the rock. Then he rolled a huge stone across the entrance to the tomb and departed.
Matthew 27: 57-60

Moment of Silence

Story:

I make a point of apologizing to people I have hurt in the past. I find it a crucial point of development and karmic cleansing. More often than not, people tell me not to even worry about it but I really do think that it is important to make amends and clear the slate as much as possible to live a congruent life.

Moment of Silence

All: Living, loving Spirit, let me practice forgiveness today by starting with the little hurts. I will let go of all the everyday occurrences that do not go the way I want, and the moment I begin to feel the familiar feeling of anger or resentment, I will practice forgiveness by invoking your loving and peaceful Presence and allowing divine grace to surround me. And so it is..

The Lord's Prayer

Our Father, which art in heaven,
Hallowed be thy Name.
Thy Kingdom come.
Thy will be done on earth,
As it is in heaven.
Give us this day our daily bread.
And forgive us our trespasses,
As we forgive them that trespass against us.
And lead us not into temptation,
But deliver us from evil.
For thine is the kingdom,
The power, and the glory,
For ever and ever.
Amen.

The Apostles' Creed

I believe in God, the Father Almighty,
the Maker of heaven and earth,
and in Jesus Christ, His only Son, our Lord:
Who was conceived by the Holy Ghost,
born of the virgin Mary,
suffered under Pontius Pilate,
was crucified, dead, and buried;
He descended into hell.
The third day He arose again from the dead;
He ascended into heaven,
and sitteth on the right hand of God the Father Almighty;
from thence he shall come to judge the quick and the dead.
I believe in the Holy Ghost;
the holy catholic church;
the communion of saints;
the forgiveness of sins;
the resurrection of the body;
and the life everlasting.
Amen.

Stations Of The Cross

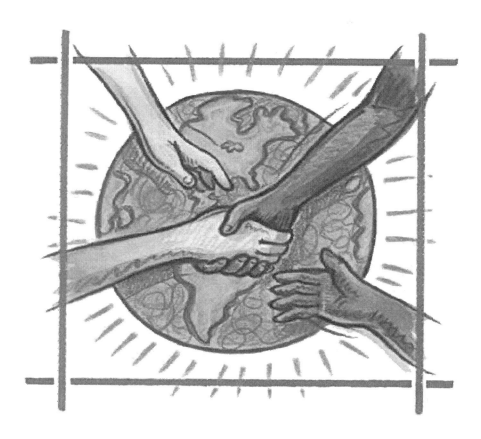

This Land Was Made For You And Me

By Earl Clinton Williams, Jr.

Acclamations

What you are about to read and experience will hopefully of those that immigrated from other countries and why they came.

I would like to thank my parents, my sister, my nephews, my relatives, friends, the Episcopal Church, and the Quakers, along with many others who helped me become the person that I am.

I would also like to give thanks to the Holy Trinity in guiding me through the process of putting this together. I only hope and pray that this is an instrument that will help this world become a better place.

Station 1: Jesus in the Garden of Gethsemane

-

Leader: We adore you, oh Christ, and we bless you.
All: **Because by your holy cross you have redeemed the world.**

Reading:

Then Jesus came with them to a place called Gethsemane, and he said to his disciples, "Sit here while I go over there and pray." He took along Peter and the two sons of Zebedee, and began to feel sorrow and distress. Then he said to them, "My soul is sorrowful even to death. Remain here and keep watch with me." He advanced a little and fell prostrate in prayer, saying, "My Father, if it is possible, let this cup pass from me; yet, not as I will, but as you will." When he returned to his disciples he found them asleep. He said to Peter, "So you could not keep watch with me for one hour? Watch and pray that you may not undergo the test. The spirit is willing, but the flesh is weak."
Matthew 25:36-41

Moment of Silence

Story:

I am an immigrant several times over. I've lived in the US for 9 years, but I hold Russian and UK passports.

To get our greencards - which took much longer than usual - we had to submit to an interview (with a lawyer present!), which isn't normal procedure. They naturally asked my parents if they were Communists (since you had to be part of the Komsomol to go to college in Russia, they had been marked as "affiliated" with the party), but then the official, in all seriousness, asked *me* if I had been affiliated.

I was 1 year old when the Communist regime tumbled down.

McCarthyism a tad perhaps?

Moment of Silence

All: Father I ask that you stay at the center of my life. I ask that you guide me through my day and be with me every step of the way. Give me strength and help me to overcome the obstacles that are placed before me with the help of thy word and thy grace. Watch over us,keep us in thy safe keeping ,keep us free from the clutches of the adversary. deliver us from evil and forgive us when we fall short. Help us to do thy will..

Station 2: Jesus, Betrayed by Judas, is Arrested

Leader: We adore you, oh Christ, and we bless you.
All: **Because by your holy cross you have redeemed the world.**

Reading:

Then, while [Jesus] was still speaking, Judas, one of the Twelve, arrived, accompanied by a crowd with swords and clubs, who had come from the chief priests, the scribes, and the elders. His betrayer had arranged a signal with them, saying, "the man I shall kiss is the one; arrest him and lead him away securely." He came and immediately went over to him and said, "Rabbi." And he kissed him. At this they laid hands on him and arrested him.
Mark 14: 43-46

Moment of Silence

Story:

My experience began almost two years ago when my I applied for my husband citizenship. My real struggle didn't actual begin until four months ago (January 2011). In January my husband received an appointment (out of country) for an interview on behalf of his life here in the United States. After the interview they found him unable to be approved for a visa, which would grant him to return home. See when my husband was 4 yrs old his parents brought him to the U.S. illegally and they never applied to become citizens. Because he lived in the U.S. for 21 years illegally, they had to deny him. This could come at a worse time for us: I just had my first baby and he was about to receive a promotion at work. I went with my husband to his appointment, and was able to spend five days with him locked up in a hotel. Those would become the last five days I spent with him in months. When I came home I was thrown into a battle with raising a newborn son, maintaining a household, caring for a stepson, working 10 hr days- when I could, and going back and forth with immigration. The first month was the worst. I made very little money and couldn't afford to go grocery shopping for 5 weeks. I eventually lost the home I was renting. Ever since then I've been doing all I can to stay strong and get my husband home. To be honest I can say, today anyways, I'm okay!

Moment of Silence

All: Father I ask that you stay at the center of my life. I ask that you guide me through my day and be with me every step of the way. Give me strength and help me to overcome the obstacles that are placed before me with the help of thy word and thy grace. Watch over us,keep us in thy safe keeping ,keep us free from the clutches of the adversary. deliver us from evil and forgive us when we fall short. Help us to do thy will.

Station 3: Jesus is Condemned by the Sanhedrin

Leader: We adore you, oh Christ, and we bless you.
All: **Because by your holy cross you have redeemed the world.**

Reading:

When day came the council of elders of the people met, both chief priests and scribes, and they brought him before their Sanhedrin. They said, "If you are the Messiah, tell us," but he replied to them, "If I tell you, you will not believe, and if I question, you will not respond. But from this time on the Son of Man will be seated at the right hand of the power of God." They all asked, "Are you then the Son of God?" He replied to them, "You say that I am." Then they said, "What further need have we for testimony? We have heard it from his own mouth."
Luke 22: 66-71

Moment of Silence

Story:

When my parents got married, almost 16 years ago, they were planning on moving to the U.S, though at the time it was a little harder so they waited a few years and then immigrated to America.

My Moms parents had just recently moved to America, about 3 years before my parents did. When I was 2, we went to Japan (where my Dad is from) to visit my other grandparents (Dads parents) and while we were there my Moms Father fell ill and soon past away. We had to cut our visit short so we could make it to his funeral. But when we were at the airport, they said there was a problem with the papers my parents had signed when they first moved to the U.S, and therefor, somehow, there was also a problem with the passports. We weren't allowed to go back until the papers had been re-signed and finalized which could have taken up to 2 months, longer if they didn't have passports. My Mom was heartbroken, she was begging them to let her go back because she wanted to be at her fathers funeral, but they wouldn't let her, they didn't even seem to care. My parents were horrified that these people didn't seem to care one bit. We never got back in time and we missed my Grandads funeral.

The problem they found with the papers my parents signed, wasn't even my parents fault. It was who ever finalizes the papers fault if they had been more careful, there would have been no problems. Plus, since there was a problem, it turned out that we weren't official citizens and my parents were given the choice to either properly finalize the papers to become citizens, or finalize it so we could stay long enough to stay in the country to get our stuff and leave.

My parents chose to finalize it just enough to say goodbye to everyone and sell our house. Which took a little under 4 months. Less than a year later, we moved to Australia, and after a year we had the full papers signed and finalized to become Australian citizens. That was 13 years ago now. My grandma still lives in the U.S and we visit every now and then, but my parents are really paranoid now since then.

Moment of Silence

All: Father I ask that you stay at the center of my life. I ask that you guide me through my day and be with me every step of the way. Give me strength and help me to overcome the obstacles that are placed before me with the help of thy word and thy grace. Watch over us,keep us in thy safe keeping ,keep us free from the clutches of the adversary. deliver us from evil and forgive us when we fall short. Help us to do thy will..

Station 4: Jesus is Denied by Peter

Leader: We adore you, oh Christ, and we bless you.
All: **Because by your holy cross you have redeemed the world.**

Reading:

Now Peter was sitting outside in the courtyard. One of the maids came over to him and said, "You too were with Jesus the Galilean." But he denied it in front of everyone, saying, "I do not know what you are talking about!" As he went out to the gate, another girl saw him and said to those who were there, "This man was with Jesus the Nazorean." Again he denied it with an oath, "I do not know the man!" A little later the bystanders came over and said to Peter, "Surely you too are one of them; even your speech gives you away." At that he began to curse and to swear, "I do not know the man." And immediately a cock crowed. Then Peter remembered the word that Jesus had spoken: "Before the cock crows you will deny me three times." He went out and began to weep bitterly.
Matthew 26: 69-75

Moment of Silence

Story:

When everything is blamed on immigrants. Crime, unemployment, litter, you name it, it's our fault. Yes, we came here and ruined everything. Because you NEVER did anything bad did you? You've been 100% law-abiding and altruistic to your fellow citizens since birth. You've never claimed welfare, you've never tried to avoid taxes. You've never had a day off on false pretenses. You've never scrawled graffiti on a wall, or thrown an empty can from a car. You are so angelic you should have a halo. Before we came your country was perfect, like a wonderland, with happy smiling people sharing everything and loving one another, never fighting, never looking down on anyone. Now it's a hellhole where it's not safe to walk the streets at night because we roam in gangs looking for innocent strangers to attack. Yep, that's us. We savages came here to destroy your culture. We thought that would be a really good idea, as we wanted to live in a post-apocalyptic society. We thought we'd like to turn your land into a wasteland, and then raise our children in that. Because we hate our children, you know?

Moment of Silence

All: Father I ask that you stay at the center of my life. I ask that you guide me through my day and be with me every step of the way. Give me strength and help me to overcome the obstacles that are placed before me with the help of thy word and thy grace. Watch over us,keep us in thy safe keeping ,keep us free from the clutches of the adversary. deliver us from evil and forgive us when we fall short. Help us to do thy will..

Station 5: Jesus is Judged by Pilate

Leader: We adore you, oh Christ, and we bless you.
All: **Because by your holy cross you have redeemed the world.**

Reading:

The chief priests with the elders and the scribes, that is, the whole Sanhedrin, held a council. They bound Jesus, led him away, and handed him over to Pilate. Pilate questioned him, "Are you the king of the Jews?" He said to him in reply, "You say so." The chief priests accused him of many things. Again Pilate questioned him, "Have you no answer? See how many things they accuse you of." Jesus gave him no further answer, so that Pilate was amazed.... Pilate, wishing to satisfy the crowd, released Barrabas... [and] handed [Jesus] over to be crucified.
Mark 15: 1-5, 15

Moment of Silence

Story:

Nice, perhaps they "Americans" feel that way because that's what they did to the true Americans, the American Indians. Most Caucasian Americans who support this whole immigration right wing movement are ignorant to the fact that it's not only Mexicans who are immigrants. I especially love that they practically witch hunt the Mexican race, when there are Polish, German, Russian immigrants here illegally just to name the "white" immigrants, but hey they're OK, they're not Mexican. Also, the Al-Quida immigrants who continue to pass here illegally, but they must be coming from the Mexico border that's why we need a fence. Remember it was the Mexican's who attacked America on her on soil right? It was the Mexican's who cost American thousands of lives. Whenever you're opposed by anyone spitting the ignorance of this immigrant witch hunt, just respond to them simply by saying, oh, you must be an American Indian, because they are the only ones who didn't migrate here from another country. America is who she is BECAUSE of all the immigrants who came here looking for the same goal, a goal that can only be denied to who? You got it, the Mexicans!

Moment of Silence

All: Father I ask that you stay at the center of my life. I ask that you guide me through my day and be with me every step of the way. Give me strength and help me to overcome the obstacles that are placed before me with the help of thy word and thy grace. Watch over us,keep us in thy safe keeping ,keep us free from the clutches of the adversary. deliver us from evil and forgive us when we fall short. Help us to do thy will..

Station 6: Jesus is Scourged and Crowned with Thorns

Leader: We adore you, oh Christ, and we bless you.
All: **Because by your holy cross you have redeemed the world.**

Reading:

Then Pilate took Jesus and had him scourged. And the soldiers wove a crown out of thorns and placed it on his head, and clothed him in a purple cloak, and they came to him and said,"Hail, King of the Jews!" And they struck him repeatedly.

John 19: 1-3

Moment of Silence

Here is my tragic life story. I was born in some non-EU place, I never had any family and grew in foster care. since I was a child I resented the country I lived, their language, culture, everything. I felt like an alien, and never fit in any company of local people. I read books since I was 3 yo, trying to find out where I belonged too, but nothing clicked.. the country was poor, but I married a successful man, got a good job, had a nice apartment. still it never changed the way I felt, I was depressed and unhappy and all I wanted was to leave that place forever. money didn't matter much for me, I just wanted to find the place and circle of people I'd be comfortable with..

At some stage something clicked. thru the football team I started to support for unknown even for me reasons, I found my dream country. Went there for holidays, it was extremely hard to get visa, but I had a good job, rich husband so I got it.

It was exactly what I dreamed of, I finally found this place where I felt at home at last. but there was no chance for me to ever ever move there legally. I developed nervous breakdown when I came back. I couldn't stand the sound of the local language, the only people I spoke to were English speakers... I grew apart from me husband, he didn't want to move anywhere, he loved his country, but I started to feel desperate.

Then one day I managed to get a holiday visa and fled. I was going to commit suicide if I failed. I simply couldn't take that life anymore, I wanted to be with my own people even for some time before I would have to die.

I run away with nothing, though I was pretty rich in that country. I got some EU papers, so I got a job, but I didn't think of lots of complications... I never got a birth certificate for example, so I cant fill any forms if I'm sick for example. they require the mother's maiden name, and how would I know it.. not one of me mates can help me to find it out... so I'm screwed, I never committed any crime in my life, always worked hard and payed tax. My only fault was that I was born in some place I never wanted to be.

Now I'm depressed and thinking of suicide. I saw the life it should be, but I can only watch it. With no papers I cant go on holidays, I cant get married, I cant start a family, or buy a house. it will never happen. my life is wasted just because I wasn't born in EU.

If I commit suicide I wont hurt anyone. as I said I never had any family and I couldn't afford close friends either. they would ask questions, and I wouldn't be able to give them any answers. so I'm on my own, suffer from panic attacks and nightmares, which always about going back to that place I fled from...there's no miracle for me, I cant imagine what I would need as a miracle... its no even chance to get that mothers maiden name... all I ever wanted is to have a simply life, with just enough money, and a nice fella to be with. instead I live in a squat, and the only fellas I ever met, were chronic alcoholics and addicts, what else could I expect in my situation., nobody else would be interested to be involved in a such messed up life..

Well that's my story. maybe someone has something to say about it... I would like to know what people might think of such weird true life story...

Moment of Silence

All: Father I ask that you stay at the center of my life. I ask that you guide me through my day and be with me every step of the way. Give me strength and help me to overcome the obstacles that are placed before me with the help of thy word and thy grace. Watch over us,keep us in thy safe keeping ,keep us free from the clutches of the adversary. deliver us from evil and forgive us when we fall short. Help us to do thy will..

Station 7: Jesus Bears the Cross

Leader: We adore you, oh Christ, and we bless you.
All: **Because by your holy cross you have redeemed the world.**

Reading:

When the chief priests and the guards saw [Jesus] they cried out, "Crucify him, crucify him!" Pilate said to them, "Take him yourselves and crucify him. I find no guilt in him." ... They cried out, "Take him away, take him away! Crucify him!" Pilate said to them, "Shall I crucify your king?" The chief priests answered, "We have no king but Caesar." Then he handed him over to them to be crucified. So they took Jesus, and carrying the cross himself he went out to what is called the Place of the Skull, in Hebrew,Golgotha.
John 19: 6, 15-17

Moment of Silence

Story:

OK. This one of the major rants I have. I live in Alabama. Yea yea yea... I hear the snickering. Yes I have been accused of being a witch, Satanist, everything above because I am a liberal non-denominational spiritual person. I don't label myself. So therefore, I will speak freely.

What I see a lot is "THE SOUTH WILL RISE AGAIN."

So that stems from racism. Another vice. Immigration. Similar but I am getting to my point.

Immigration. I have gotten (unfortunately) to witness how rude, bigoted (is that a word?), heartless, and so on people can be!

I am the mother of biracial children. They are a dinner plate of races mixed together (isn't everyone?). Native American, Romanian, Latina (Mayan roots).

But the thing I hear secondly is "ZOOMG THESE HISPANIC FOLKZEZ ARE TAKING ALL OUR JOBS THEY NEEDZ TO GO BACK HOMEZ!!"

OK. I would like for someone to PLEASE tell me who owned the US before it was even CONSIDERED the US? Who LIVED here before the "white man" came? Indians.

Indians. The Cherokee, Choctaw, and on and on and on.... The cousins of the Mayas, Aztecs, and so on.

So quit with your "get out of here and go home" BS. They ARE home.

Moment of Silence

All: Father I ask that you stay at the center of my life. I ask that you guide me through my day and be with me every step of the way. Give me strength and help me to overcome the obstacles that are placed before me with the help of thy word and thy grace. Watch over us,keep us in thy safe keeping ,keep us free from the clutches of the adversary. deliver us from evil and forgive us when we fall short. Help us to do thy will.

Station 8: Jesus is Helped by Simon the Cyrenian to Carry the Cross

Leader: We adore you, oh Christ, and we bless you.
All: **Because by your holy cross you have redeemed the world.**

Reading:

They pressed into service a passer-by, Simon, a Cyrenian, who was coming in from the country, the father of Alexander and Rufus, to carry his cross.
Mark 15: 21

Moment of Silence

Story:

I grew up in New York City, where people are of any and every ethnic heritage imaginable. I had always heard about prejudice, bigotry, and racism, but growing up on the lower east side in the 50s and 60s had no real idea what people were talking about.

Then at the age of 30, I moved to Massachusetts, a state which has the reputation of being accepting, liberal, tolerant, etc. etc. and is actually the most bigoted, racist, hateful place I've ever been in my life (and I live in the south now). I lived at first in Boston, and for the first time I heard people (almost exclusively white people) speak of "us" and "them." There were certain neighborhoods where it was dangerous for me to go. The signs in public places were all exclusively in English--I was used to English, Spanish, Hebrew, and Russian in NYC. Everyplace I went in Boston everybody looked the same, dressed the same, ate the same food, and assumed that was fine with everyone else. In the town of Melrose in 1978 (the year I moved there from the city of Boston), there was only ONE person of African descent in a city of 34,000 people: he and his wife were the parents of the only two biracial children in the Melrose public school system! What a ghastly place Melrose was. I couldn't get out of there fast enough.

Later on I lived on the north shore, in a community that was largely non-white--Puerto Rican, Dominican, Brazilian, Cambodian, and Vietnamese people far outnumbered the white people who lived there. But all you heard from white people was how "they" should stop moving into "our" country and taking away "our" jobs and ruining "our" culture. What culture is this? The white people came to this country and brutalized, raped, burned, pillaged, tortured, and murdered vast numbers of the native population here (in the name of "religious freedom", what a kicker that is!) and now want every one else to leave? This is something to be proud
                                                                                                of??!

I've never understood any of this, and I guess I never will. The funny thing is that I am descended from one of the original families that actually did come over on the Mayflower. Far from being proud of my heritage, I'm ashamed of what my ancestors did.

Moment of Silence

All: Father I ask that you stay at the center of my life. I ask that you guide me through my day and be with me every step of the way. Give me strength and help me to overcome the obstacles that are placed before me with the help of thy word and thy grace. Watch over us,keep us in thy safe keeping ,keep us free from the clutches of the adversary. deliver us from evil and forgive us when we fall short. Help us to do thy will..

Station 9: Jesus Meets the Women of Jerusalem

Leader: We adore you, oh Christ, and we bless you.
All: **Because by your holy cross you have redeemed the world.**

Reading:

A large crowd of people followed Jesus, including many women who mourned and lamented him. Jesus turned to them and said, "Daughters of Jerusalem, do not weep for me; weep instead for yourselves and for your children, for indeed, the days are coming when people will say, 'Blessed are the barren, the wombs that never bore and the breasts that never nursed.' At that time, people will say to the mountains, 'Fall upon us!' and to the hills, 'Cover us!' for if these things are done when the wood is green what will happen when it is dry?"
Luke 23: 27-31

Moment of Silence

Story:

So, I was in this class in High School where we'd have mock congressional hearings about parts of the Constitution of the United States.

One of the topics that almost always came up was Illegal Immigration.

The first time we discussed it as a class, I brought up the point that technically, none of us were truly 'native' to the land and that under this concept, we are all immigrants. The class all stared at me, then at each other, then back at me, before this one kid (the one who decided to bring up an idea to just close all our borders and let NO immigrants in) laughed and told me that was dumb.

I stared at him before replying something along the lines of America being born on the idea that we were a 'mixing pot' for immigration and that one of the biggest reasons we were so successful as a nation was found in the fact that so many heritages were mixed together in our national community.

Needless to say, at the time, the class just laughed at me and sided with the guy because he was popular. The next week, our teacher reaffirmed my remarks in her lecture and the guy was laughed at for being so naive.

That class was fun. :)

Moment of Silence

All: Father I ask that you stay at the center of my life. I ask that you guide me through my day and be with me every step of the way. Give me strength and help me to overcome the obstacles that are placed before me with the help of thy word and thy grace. Watch over us,keep us in thy safe keeping ,keep us free from the clutches of the adversary. deliver us from evil and forgive us when we fall short. Help us to do thy will..

Station 10: Jesus is Crucified

Leader: We adore you, oh Christ, and we bless you.
All: **Because by your holy cross you have redeemed the world.**

Reading:

When they came to the place called the Skull, they crucified him and the criminals there, one on his right, the other on his left. [Then Jesus said, "Father, forgive them, they know not what they do."] *Luke 23: 33-34*

Moment of Silence

Story:

I was with my kids father since 2001 and we have 2 children together. He went to work in California to make a better life for us and we turned in all the correct papers. He went to his court date and from court they gave him a paper saying his papers has been accepted but yet he was on his way back here to Louisiana, ICE pulled him off the bus and arrested him and said that was not a legal document. So they deported him back to Mexico and now we are fighting for his papers. A lawyer in New Orleans said we have a good case because it is a legal document that was signed by the immigration courts. His rights to be here are legal and I have been writing to the congress to help me but no word yet. It's been almost a year. I have a special needs child and another child that is dealing with separation anxiety and my oldest went to Mexico to visit his father and know I may have troubles bringing my son back across the border. He is an American citizen and I just want my kids father back and my son back as well. I miss them a lot. Te amo mucho mi amor. Aqui estoy esperando a ti con toda corazon.

Moment of Silence

All: Father I ask that you stay at the center of my life. I ask that you guide me through my day and be with me every step of the way. Give me strength and help me to overcome the obstacles that are placed before me with the help of thy word and thy grace. Watch over us,keep us in thy safe keeping ,keep us free from the clutches of the adversary. deliver us from evil and forgive us when we fall short. Help us to do thy will..

Station 11: Jesus Promises His Kingdom to the Good Thief

Leader: We adore you, oh Christ, and we bless you.

All: **Because by your holy cross you have redeemed the world.**

Reading:

Now one of the criminals hanging there reviled Jesus, saying, "Are you not the Messiah? Save yourself and us." The other, however, rebuking him, said in reply, "Have you no fear of God, for you are subject to the same condemnation? And indeed, we have been condemned justly, for the sentence we received corresponds to our crimes, but this man has done nothing criminal." Then he said, "Jesus, remember me when you come into your kingdom." He replied to him, "Amen, I say to you, today you will be with me in Paradise."
Luke 23: 39-43

Moment of Silence

Story:

This is the story of my fiance Maria. She has been in the States since 1991. She is from the Philippines. This Immigration problem is still going on. She is a victim of the Motor Voter law. She went to the DMV in 2003 to get a State ID and she showed her Permanent Resident card as a form of ID. She proceeded to get her State ID and then was asked if she would like to register to vote. She did not know that she couldn't vote, so she registered and voted one time in 2004. The form she signed was already completed. The questions on it that ask if you are a citizen do not have boxes to check Yes or No. The DMV employee just pushed it in front of her and said sign. By the way this form was changed in 2004 because of this problem. In 2007 she applied for citizenship and told the truth that she voted. Her citizenship was denied in 2008 and she was put in removal proceedings for voting one time. She told the truth and now she could be deported for a mistake. This kind of thing happens a lot and Immigration will say we do not care how this happened, you did something wrong. Yes but it was not her intention. She made an innocent mistake because the DMV has to asked everyone citizen or not to register to vote, and if you are not a citizen and you do not know that you cannot vote.

Moment of Silence

All: Father I ask that you stay at the center of my life. I ask that you guide me through my day and be with me every step of the way. Give me strength and help me to overcome the obstacles that are placed before me with the help of thy word and thy grace. Watch over us,keep us in thy safe keeping ,keep us free from the clutches of the adversary. deliver us from evil and forgive us when we fall short. Help us to do thy will..

Station 12: Jesus Speaks to His Mother and the Disciple

Leader: We adore you, oh Christ, and we bless you.
All: **Because by your holy cross you have redeemed the world.**

Reading:

Standing by the cross of Jesus were his mother and his mother's sister, Mary the wife of Clopas, and Mary of Magdala. When Jesus saw his mother and the disciple there whom he loved, he said to his mother, "Woman, behold, your son." Then he said to the disciple, "Behold, your mother." And from that hour the disciple took her into his home.
John 19: 25-27

Moment of Silence

Story:

I'm 19 and everyday I think to myself if I wasn't "illegal" I'd be somebody right now. I came here when I was 1 year old. I didn't even know I was illegal till I was in fifth grade. All I spoke was English and was in gifted and talented classes. In fifth grade I went to a charter school where I worked my butt off to earn a trip to Washington D.C and I did. I went to the Smithsonian and the capital, Arlington Cemetery, I even met a senator who met and was inspired by The Rev. Dr. Martin Luther King, Jr.. The day came where I would visit the White House, and it was the happiest day of short life as a fifth grader. I was held back as my teacher explained to me that I wasn't allowed in because I was different. And I cried on the steps outside of the building. I called my mom and she told me I was illegal. But that didn't stop me. I've been to Philadelphia, California, New York, Utah, Chicago. All with my intelligence. I went to college in high school because I finished early. I participated in plays because I love acting, and have been asked to model. But after my 18th birthday I realized I couldn't keep going. I graduated from high school and managed to get college credits too. Things were harder in the real world. I couldn't never pay for college. And even if I was born in Mexico, I have the American culture in me. I can tell you the 50 capital and states, tell you the American history since Plymouth Rock. And I'm not holding a grudge. If I couldn't do it all, one day my kids will. And even if I'm not legal I know I'm a model citizen, and a good person. I didn't choose this but I trust in God. I still envy people that have social security. They don't know what they have. They have a chance. You would never guess my dilemma if you saw me walking down the street. A young beautiful smart gal, you'd think I would have it all. But I don't, until then I live my humble life.

Moment of Silence

All: Father I ask that you stay at the center of my life. I ask that you guide me through my day and be with me every step of the way. Give me strength and help me to overcome the obstacles that are placed before me with the help of thy word and thy grace. Watch over us,keep us in thy safe keeping ,keep us free from the clutches of the adversary. deliver us from evil and forgive us when we fall short. Help us to do thy will..

Station 13: Jesus Dies on the Cross

Leader: We adore you, oh Christ, and we bless you.
All: **Because by your holy cross you have redeemed the world.**

Reading:

It was now about noon and darkness came over the whole land until three in the afternoon because of an eclipse of the sun. Then the veil of the temple was torn down the middle. Jesus cried out in a loud voice, "Father, into your hands I commend my spirit"; and when he had said this he breathed his last. *Luke 23: 44-46*

Moment of Silence

Story:

I moved to the United States in 1977 at the age of 2 with my family from Canada. When I was 18 I did some stupid things and ended up having to serve 35 days in jail and two years of probation. Since then I have made huge changes in my life and haven't even had a speeding ticket since 1996. This past spring I had to travel back to Canada for a family funeral. When I tried to return to the states I was detained at the border because of my criminal record. Customs officers confiscated my green card, took my fingerprints and my mug shot. They then took several hours to fill out all the correct paperwork before they paroled me into the country. I have crossed that border countless times since my arrest as a teen and this was the first time I have ever had any trouble returning to the states. Now I am facing deportation because of a mistake I made nearly 20 years ago. I have had to pay out $4000 to an attorney plus several hundreds of dollars in filing fees for applications just to stay in this country with my family. I recently had to appear in immigration court for my preliminary hearing. My new court date is set for SIX MONTHS from now! The temporary green card that was issued to me expires two months before my rescheduled hearing. This means that I will have to apply for yet another temporary green card. I am convinced that this is nothing more than extortion by the United States government. Not only extortion of money but of my time as well. This entire process has made me bitter and very unhappy with this country. How is it that a productive and responsible adult that hasn't broken any laws in nearly 20 years has to prove themselves worthy of living in this country while there are people out there like many celebrities than can travel in and out of this country without any trouble and continue to thumb their noses at the judicial system?

Moment of Silence

All: Father I ask that you stay at the center of my life. I ask that you guide me through my day and be with me every step of the way. Give me strength and help me to overcome the obstacles that are placed before me with the help of thy word and thy grace. Watch over us,keep us in thy safe keeping ,keep us free from the clutches of the adversary. deliver us from evil and forgive us when we fall short. Help us to do thy will.

Station 14: Jesus is Placed in the Tomb

Leader: We adore you, oh Christ, and we bless you.

All: **Because by your holy cross you have redeemed the world.**

Reading:

When it was evening, there came a rich man from Arimathea named Joseph, who was himself a disciple of Jesus. He went to Pilate and asked for the body of Jesus; then Pilate ordered it to be handed over. Taking the body, Joseph wrapped it [in] clean linen and laid it in his new tomb that he had hewn in the rock. Then he rolled a huge stone across the entrance to the tomb and departed. *Matthew 27: 57-60*

Moment of Silence

Story:

I came to the U.S when I was 8 months. My parents are both immigrants from Egypt. They lived in Cairo, Egypt for a while then they moved to Mexico where my dad had family members. I was born there and 3 months after I was born my father died. In Mexico my mom met my step dad who I thought was my dad until recently. When I was 8 months we came to the U.S. My dream had always been to become a Marine like my step grandfather was and my older brothers and sister. They are all dead. Aaron died recently in Afghanistan. He's the bravest person I've ever met. But because I am "illegal" here I cant become a Marine until I become a resident of the U.S. or a citizen. But recently I learned that if I apply as soon as I turn 18 I might be able to qualify. I hope so. It's my dream.

Moment of Silence

All: Father I ask that you stay at the center of my life. I ask that you guide me through my day and be with me every step of the way. Give me strength and help me to overcome the obstacles that are placed before me with the help of thy word and thy grace. Watch over us,keep us in thy safe keeping ,keep us free from the clutches of the adversary. deliver us from evil and forgive us when we fall short. Help us to do thy will..

Stations Of The Cross

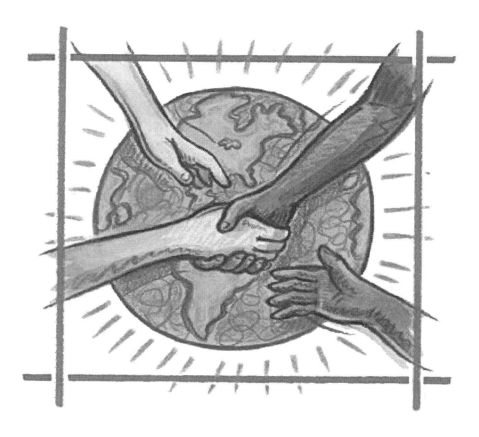

A Centered Life

By Earl Clinton Williams, Jr.

Acclamations

What you are about to read and experience will hopefully bring you to a closer Center with the Holy Trinity.

I would like to thank my parents, my sister, my nephews, my relatives, friends, the Episcopal Church, and the Quakers, along with many others who helped me become the person that I am.

I would also like to give thanks to the Holy Trinity in guiding me through the process of putting this together. I only hope and pray that this is an instrument that will help this world become a better place.

Station 1: Jesus in the Garden of Gethsemane

-

Leader: We adore you, oh Christ, and we bless you.
All: **Because by your holy cross you have redeemed the world.**

Reading:

Then Jesus came with them to a place called Gethsemane, and he said to his disciples, "Sit here while I go over there and pray." He took along Peter and the two sons of Zebedee, and began to feel sorrow and distress. Then he said to them, "My soul is sorrowful even to death. Remain here and keep watch with me." He advanced a little and fell prostrate in prayer, saying, "My Father, if it is possible, let this cup pass from me; yet, not as I will, but as you will." When he returned to his disciples he found them asleep. He said to Peter, "So you could not keep watch with me for one hour? Watch and pray that you may not undergo the test. The spirit is willing, but the flesh is weak."
Matthew 25:36-41

Moment of Silence

Story:

Hopefully I Can Keep Him There

There's been times in my life when I'd convinced myself that I had put God above all else , only to learn that it wasn't true . When put to the test , I often had myself on a much higher pedestal . It doesn't work that way . God is to be the center of my personal universe and when my walk with Him has been close , life has been good and rewarding for me and all those around me . I know that anytime I choose to ,He'll be near to listen to my prayer and guide me on the straight and narrow paths that lead to righteousness . Help me , O Lord , to open my heart unto you and never to turn my back on you again .

Moment of Silence

All: Father I ask that you stay at the center of my life. I ask that you guide me through my day and be with me every step of the way. Give me strength and help me to overcome the obstacles that are placed before me with the help of thy word and thy grace. Watch over us,keep us in thy safe keeping ,keep us free from the clutches of the adversary. deliver us from evil and forgive us when we fall short. Help us to do thy will..

Station 2: Jesus, Betrayed by Judas, is Arrested

Leader: We adore you, oh Christ, and we bless you.
All: **Because by your holy cross you have redeemed the world.**

Reading:

Then, while [Jesus] was still speaking, Judas, one of the Twelve, arrived, accompanied by a crowd with swords and clubs, who had come from the chief priests, the scribes, and the elders. His betrayer had arranged a signal with them, saying, "the man I shall kiss is the one; arrest him and lead him away securely." He came and immediately went over to him and said, "Rabbi." And he kissed him. At this they laid hands on him and arrested him.
Mark 14: 43-46

Moment of Silence

Story:

My Goal: To Be A Stronger Christian

As I sit here tonight, (Good Friday) I have hopes of a day where I don't struggle with temptations. And, for Christians, this day will come for all of us. It will be the day when God calls us home. For, we will all, as God's followers, deal with, and face temptation head on for as long as we have breath in our body.

I want to be a better Christian. I want to stand bold with Christ. I want to clothe myself in Spiritual armor. Let us turn to, in the King James Version of the Holy Bible, the Book of Ephesians, written by the Apostle Paul. Find the Armor of God in chapter 6, verses 11-17.

For my new friend who shares the same struggles as I do, find in verse 11, "Put on the whole armor of God, that ye may be able to stand against the wiles of the devil." Take comfort that you are not alone.

The armor of God, according to the Apostle Paul: (emphasis, mine)
- Gird your loins with **truth**
- * **Breastplate** of **righteousness**
- * Your feet shod with **preparation of the Gospel of Peace**
- * Take the **shield** of **faith**
- * The **helmet** of **Salvation**
- * **Sword of the Spirit**, which **IS THE WORD OF GOD**

Arm yourselves with these things so that "ye may be able to withstand the evil day, and having done all, to stand," says Paul in verse 13 of Chapter 6--Book of Ephesians.

Moment of Silence

All: Father I ask that you stay at the center of my life. I ask that you guide me through my day and be with me every step of the way. Give me strength and help me to overcome the obstacles that are placed before me with the help of thy word and thy grace. Watch over us,keep us in thy safe keeping ,keep us free from the clutches of the adversary. deliver us from evil and forgive us when we fall short. Help us to do thy will..

Station 3: Jesus is Condemned by the Sanhedrin

Leader: We adore you, oh Christ, and we bless you.

All: **Because by your holy cross you have redeemed the world.**

Reading:

When day came the council of elders of the people met, both chief priests and scribes, and they brought him before their Sanhedrin. They said, "If you are the Messiah, tell us," but he replied to them, "If I tell you, you will not believe, and if I question, you will not respond. But from this time on the Son of Man will be seated at the right hand of the power of God." They all asked, "Are you then the Son of God?" He replied to them, "You say that I am." Then they said, "What further need have we for testimony? We have heard it from his own mouth."
Luke 22: 66-71

Moment of Silence

Story:

Maybe I Don't Need To Be A Better Christians

In the Lutheran Church we have an Individual Order of Confession where we merely tell God that we want to do better. We don't ask God to make us super Christians who are a walking embodiment of Jesus. While I am not gay I ask people why my brother, who is gay, is wrong in going to a Lutheran Church every Sunday even though he has no interest in being cured of the gay. They say that they don't allow people who gossip to go to their churches because one has to be Christ like to be welcome in a church. Maybe they are right, but if you are an alcoholic do they tell you not to go to church until you are sober?

I just don't understand this need to be a better Christian. Jesus said to come as you are and that is what I do. Not to brag, but I suppose I'm a better Christian now in that I am more patient and accepting of people and such. Maybe its because I accepted Jesus as my Lord and Savior when I was six that I didn't learn to hate and hold grudges. I began with the Lord's Prayer which says that if we don't forgive others then God really doesn't need to forgive us because that's what we ask him to do. To forgive us in the same manner and extent as we forgive others.

While I can disapprove of someone's behavior I cannot judge them in or our of Heaven. To do that I would need to crawl up on God's Throne and become a mini-god which would then be a form of idolatry because I'm worshiping myself instead of God. Still, people are quick to condemn my brother to hell because he's gay. So maybe if I could learn to hate my favorite brother I could be a better Christian?

So I don't know, what does it mean to be a better Christian? Are we to be better than Jesus who humbled himself and took the lowly servant's role and washed his disciples feet and took the criminal's role when he died on the cross. I cannot get that humble so I guess I will never be a better Christian.

So did Jesus die for my sins, too? Or am I not good enough for the fold? Do I really need to be a better Christian? Or is it okay that I love myself just the way I am, just trying to do better, to the same extent that God loves me which He expressed in John 3:16. Please note John 3:17.

Moment of Silence

All: Father I ask that you stay at the center of my life. I ask that you guide me through my day and be with me every step of the way. Give me strength and help me to overcome the obstacles that are placed before me with the help of thy word and thy grace. Watch over us,keep us in thy safe keeping ,keep us free from the clutches of the adversary. deliver us from evil and forgive us when we fall short. Help us to do thy will..

Station 4: Jesus is Denied by Peter

Leader: We adore you, oh Christ, and we bless you.
All: **Because by your holy cross you have redeemed the world.**

Reading:

Now Peter was sitting outside in the courtyard. One of the maids came over to him and said, "You too were with Jesus the Galilean." But he denied it in front of everyone, saying, "I do not know what you are talking about!" As he went out to the gate, another girl saw him and said to those who were there, "This man was with Jesus the Nazorean." Again he denied it with an oath, "I do not know the man!" A little later the bystanders came over and said to Peter, "Surely you too are one of them; even your speech gives you away." At that he began to curse and to swear, "I do not know the man." And immediately a cock crowed. Then Peter remembered the word that Jesus had spoken: "Before the cock crows you will deny me three times." He went out and began to weep bitterly.
Matthew 26: 69-75

Moment of Silence

Story:

I Am Blessed By God

I have held onto my Faith during the worst times over the last year and asked God to provide for me, as I couldn't find a job that would pay enough to keep my family alive. I haven't worked full time in over 15 months, so I was almost out of money, savings and retirement all spent, and things suddenly started happening that made no sense, until now. First I get some work to do from the house that pays decent money (on Friday), then someone in my men's group (Wednesday) says that God has impressed upon him that I needed special prayer to help battle the things I was going through (I was so depressed that suicide was looking better every day), and then one of the other men gives me a Psalm to read (Psalms 126) and when I read it the passage didn't make a lot of sense to me.

Then later on Wednesday, I talked to the one that said God had impressed upon him for special prayer for me and thanked him greatly, when he brought up some other things that I had been battling with. On Friday I get an email from a friend that I had been talking to about someone needing help with a special project and he needed to talk to me. On Friday night, my friend with the Psalm in his heart called me to explain it to me, although I hadn't asked for that. But on Saturday, I got a call offering me the job, at more than I had asked for, to start after the first of the year, and I would show up in North Carolina for a meeting with the principals later this week, there would also be a sign-on bonus. This was the answer to my prayers. I am truly blessed by God.

So don't lose your faith, it just takes time sometimes for God to put you on the right path... You just need to believe that he will and listen to what he is trying to tell you.

Moment of Silence

All: Father I ask that you stay at the center of my life. I ask that you guide me through my day and be with me every step of the way. Give me strength and help me to overcome the obstacles that are placed before me with the help of thy word and thy grace. Watch over us,keep us in thy safe keeping ,keep us free from the clutches of the adversary. deliver us from evil and forgive us when we fall short. Help us to do thy will..

Station 5: Jesus is Judged by Pilate

Leader: We adore you, oh Christ, and we bless you.
All: **Because by your holy cross you have redeemed the world.**

Reading:

The chief priests with the elders and the scribes, that is, the whole Sanhedrin, held a council. They bound Jesus, led him away, and handed him over to Pilate. Pilate questioned him, "Are you the king of the Jews?" He said to him in reply, "You say so." The chief priests accused him of many things. Again Pilate questioned him, "Have you no answer? See how many things they accuse you of." Jesus gave him no further answer, so that Pilate was amazed.... Pilate, wishing to satisfy the crowd, released Barrabas... [and] handed [Jesus] over to be crucified.
Mark 15: 1-5, 15

Moment of Silence

Story:

Why Is It So Hard?

Up until last semester, my first one at college, I was a very strong Christian. I spoke with God daily, I listened to what He told me and was walking on the path he had set before. But my first semester at college, I feel away. Very few of my friends were active Christians, and so I didn't have anyone to challenge me and help me grow like I'd had all throughout my life up until this point. I still tried to go to church though. That wasn't the main reason I turned away from God though. Even though I'd promised God that I wouldn't date my first semester, about 5 weeks into school I had a boyfriend. And I'm still with him. But he's a Catholic, and he had turned away from God in the past few years. I spent so much energy trying to show him God's love and how forgiving He was, and finally my boyfriend has started going to mass again and reading the Bible and his relationship with God is growing. However, over the past few months with this boyfriend, I have almost completely ignored what God has been saying to me. He tells me that I shouldn't be with my boyfriend, or should stop some things that I was doing. And I'd feel convicted at the time, but when I got back to where my boyfriend was, I'd push God out of my mind and the guilt out of my heart. By February, if not sooner, I had turned my boyfriend into an idol in my life. I had placed him as higher importance than God and valued my relationship with him over my relationship with God. I was willing to give up God to be with my boyfriend, but not vise-verso.

This past week I finally acknowledged all of this, and as scared as I was, rededicated myself to God. I thought though, that I could just put my boyfriend on the back-burner for now while I mended my relationship with God. My boyfriend is at Army basic training right now, so I miss him a lot and think about him alot. So I prayed that God would stop me from thinking about him so much and take away my temptation so that I could focus on Him. Over the past couple days since I rededicated myself, it seems that God has answered my prayers, but more than I wanted. I have rarely thought about my boyfriend, and rarely miss him, in fact I often when I think of him, its with no real feeling at all. But that doesn't mean I've been able to focus on God. I've also noticed a few other cute guys. Its like now that I don't have my boyfriend on my mind, I have to fill it with another boy instead of filling it with God! This is absolutely NOT what I wanted! I never wanted to stop thinking about my boyfriend completely, I just wanted to think about God more. And now it just hurts so bad when I think about either of them. Why does it have to be so hard to make God the center of my life? Why?! :(

Moment of Silence

All: Father I ask that you stay at the center of my life. I ask that you guide me through my day and be with me every step of the way. Give me strength and help me to overcome the obstacles that are placed before me with the help of thy word and thy grace. Watch over us,keep us in thy safe keeping ,keep us free from the clutches of the adversary. deliver us from evil and forgive us when we fall short. Help us to do thy will..

Station 6: Jesus is Scourged and Crowned with Thorns

Leader: We adore you, oh Christ, and we bless you.
All: **Because by your holy cross you have redeemed the world.**

Reading:

Then Pilate took Jesus and had him scourged. And the soldiers wove a crown out of thorns and placed it on his head, and clothed him in a purple cloak, and they came to him and said,"Hail, King of the Jews!" And they struck him repeatedly.

John 19: 1-3

Moment of Silence

Story:

We all believe in God...we all pray Him at times of trouble to help us out and keep us happy? Not just most, but all of the time He answers our prayers. But it does sometimes happen that though how much ever you pray, seems like HE ain't listening at all...your problem wouldn't seem to just vanish as it sometimes does!! Why??? Even though we trust Him so much, why doesn't He answer our prayers. Why does He let us suffer? Why does He wants to test us all of the time???

The answer is very simple! :)

You remember when you were young? Your parents sent you to school.. But they never asked you whether you like it or not. Even if you would cry not to take you to school, they would still force you.. Now, look at yourself...where you stand? you finished your studies..you are in a good position, you have the strength to stand on your own legs...you get paid. If you were not sent to school that time, would you have had all this???? :)

The same way, if God has put you in trouble and you are really not able to get over it, don't fear. Don't get angry over Him... He loves you a lot...more than your parents...more than anyone in this whole world....He would always do the best for you. So try and understand that He wants you to know something from the trouble that you have got. He wants you to be a better person in future. He wants to pull you up... He wants to take you WITH Him when you leave your body one day!! Don't ever think that He is being unfair or He is testing you over n over again. He is just trying to mold you as soon as possible ....so that you don't have to get back to earth and suffer everything all over again. Please be thankful for our LORD..!!!

THANKS FOR HEARING ME OUT MY LORD!!!

Moment of Silence

All: Father I ask that you stay at the center of my life. I ask that you guide me through my day and be with me every step of the way. Give me strength and help me to overcome the obstacles that are placed before me with the help of thy word and thy grace. Watch over us,keep us in thy safe keeping ,keep us free from the clutches of the adversary. deliver us from evil and forgive us when we fall short. Help us to do thy will..

Station 7: Jesus Bears the Cross

Leader: We adore you, oh Christ, and we bless you.
All: **Because by your holy cross you have redeemed the world.**

Reading:

When the chief priests and the guards saw [Jesus] they cried out, "Crucify him, crucify him!" Pilate said to them, "Take him yourselves and crucify him. I find no guilt in him." ... They cried out, "Take him away, take him away! Crucify him!" Pilate said to them, "Shall I crucify your king?" The chief priests answered, "We have no king but Caesar." Then he handed him over to them to be crucified. So they took Jesus, and carrying the cross himself he went out to what is called the Place of the Skull, in Hebrew,Golgotha.
John 19: 6, 15-17

Moment of Silence

Story:

Torsional

Really like the sound of that word....Just fits some days......some days are pulled and twisted. Some days with all the hustle and bustle of life it is so hard to even think that there is a center to it.....I feel scattered, strewn, directionless...clueless. Everywhere I see the day's clutter multiplying. Sometimes I'm actually deluded into thinking I can be in control....multitask..Like being on a merry go round market....Reaching out to grab things and place them in your basket without getting off the ride. Jokes on me.

When things are twisted He says He will make them straight.
When things are pulling me He says He will give me rest.
When life is cluttered and overwhelming He says be anxious for nothing. He meant "nothing".
When I am afraid He says fear not.
When I am rushed He says rest.
When I am hungry He says taste His goodness.
When I am tired He says joy comes in the morning.
When I don't know if I'm coming or going He says there is not even a shadow of changing in Him.
When I feel like the ground has become quicksand He say He's my rock.
When I worry about the uncertainty of the times He says He is Jesus Christ, the same yesterday, today and forever!

Moment of Silence

All: Father I ask that you stay at the center of my life. I ask that you guide me through my day and be with me every step of the way. Give me strength and help me to overcome the obstacles that are placed before me with the help of thy word and thy grace. Watch over us,keep us in thy safe keeping ,keep us free from the clutches of the adversary. deliver us from evil and forgive us when we fall short. Help us to do thy will..

Station 8: Jesus is Helped by Simon the Cyrenian to Carry the Cross

Leader: We adore you, oh Christ, and we bless you.
All: **Because by your holy cross you have redeemed the world.**

Reading:

They pressed into service a passer-by, Simon, a Cyrenian, who was coming in from the country, the father of Alexander and Rufus, to carry his cross.
Mark 15: 21

Moment of Silence

Story:

It's not easy. At times it is a great struggle....I strive with it....but when I keep my mental and spiritual eyes on Jesus life is so much better for me. My circumstances do not always change or improve right away but my heart lightens (He said come to me all you who are heavy laden..) and I find a strength swelling within me.

I don't always perform perfectly...I make mistakes and sin. I fall short, miss the mark and outright fail miserably at times but He is ever faithful to love and accept me.....He is constant. He says He never changes. I need to make adjustments in my thinking and actions...that is what repentance is...turning away from the wrong course of action and towards the right course......He is ever faithful with His word to guide me and direct me....when I look to Him....

He is always at the center. I'm the one who moves....goes off course ....gets sidetracked.

I can get stressed, striving to solve problems and make life better for myself. God want us to strive...strive...reach out and grasp His rest.....He is not worried, He is not anxious, He is not in a quandary or stressed out or caved in.....He is Love, Joy, Peace.....He has only that for me.....so I try to remember to work at entering His peace, trust Him and focus on the Center of all life..Jesus.

Moment of Silence

All: Father I ask that you stay at the center of my life. I ask that you guide me through my day and be with me every step of the way. Give me strength and help me to overcome the obstacles that are placed before me with the help of thy word and thy grace. Watch over us,keep us in thy safe keeping ,keep us free from the clutches of the adversary. deliver us from evil and forgive us when we fall short. Help us to do thy will..

Station 9: Jesus Meets the Women of Jerusalem

Leader: We adore you, oh Christ, and we bless you.
All: **Because by your holy cross you have redeemed the world.**

Reading:

A large crowd of people followed Jesus, including many women who mourned and lamented him. Jesus turned to them and said, "Daughters of Jerusalem, do not weep for me; weep instead for yourselves and for your children, for indeed, the days are coming when people will say, 'Blessed are the barren, the wombs that never bore and the breasts that never nursed.' At that time, people will say to the mountains, 'Fall upon us!' and to the hills, 'Cover us!' for if these things are done when the wood is green what will happen when it is dry?"
Luke 23: 27-31

Moment of Silence

Story:

I wish I could have God at the center of my life. I have realized being an average christian is not enough. Blaming others for what is wrong, or blaming circumstances will not take you anywhere. It is better to focus on God, despite all the wrongs that are going on in your life - for the weapons of our warfare are not carnal but mighty through God to the pulling down of strongholds.

Whatever situation you are going through, if you focus on God, He will give you the strength to go through it and it will pass.

Moment of Silence

All: Father I ask that you stay at the center of my life. I ask that you guide me through my day and be with me every step of the way. Give me strength and help me to overcome the obstacles that are placed before me with the help of thy word and thy grace. Watch over us,keep us in thy safe keeping ,keep us free from the clutches of the adversary. deliver us from evil and forgive us when we fall short. Help us to do thy will..

Station 10: Jesus is Crucified

Leader: We adore you, oh Christ, and we bless you.
All: **Because by your holy cross you have redeemed the world.**

Reading:

When they came to the place called the Skull, they crucified him and the criminals there, one on his right, the other on his left. [Then Jesus said, "Father, forgive them, they know not what they do."] *Luke 23: 33-34*

Moment of Silence

Story:

I've made up my mind to say the truth as God would have it said. I'm not seeking for fans or admirers because I have only one audience to please and that's the audience of the Father, Son and the Holy Ghost.

I'll Preach the whole truth not partial or half truth, I dare not be subjective or distort it with human ideas or Contemporary events, I dare not garnish it to make it appeal to individual taste or Preference because My judge on the last day would be God and not man.

People may say whatever they like, they could say I'm not modern enough; it's alright because any modernism that will make me incur the wrath of God is not worth it. I'm not ashamed for its noble call. I dare not be intimidated because the One who sent me is greater than Man.

I've made up my mind, I've counted the cost ,I've burnt the bridge behind . I'm going to be a worthy ambassador. I can't keep quiet and watch false doctrines spread everywhere; I can't be still and see multitudes perish in sin and end up in a lost eternity.

I'll defend the truth; I'll preach the whole counsel of God and not dilute it in any way. I'll tell people of God's love for humanity and, the redemption of Mankind through his son Jesus Christ and His power to save from all sinful indulgence and its guilt and make one righteous.

I'll tell everyone I see because the person I see today, I might see him/her no more. John Wesley did it, Charles G Finney did it and by Gods grace I'll do it. What about you?

Moment of Silence

All: Father I ask that you stay at the center of my life. I ask that you guide me through my day and be with me every step of the way. Give me strength and help me to overcome the obstacles that are placed before me with the help of thy word and thy grace. Watch over us,keep us in thy safe keeping ,keep us free from the clutches of the adversary. deliver us from evil and forgive us when we fall short. Help us to do thy will..

Station 11: Jesus Promises His Kingdom to the Good Thief

Leader: We adore you, oh Christ, and we bless you.

All: **Because by your holy cross you have redeemed the world.**

Reading:

 Now one of the criminals hanging there reviled Jesus, saying, "Are you not the Messiah? Save yourself and us." The other, however, rebuking him, said in reply, "Have you no fear of God, for you are subject to the same condemnation? And indeed, we have been condemned justly, for the sentence we received corresponds to our crimes, but this man has done nothing criminal." Then he said, "Jesus, remember me when you come into your kingdom." He replied to him, "Amen, I say to you, today you will be with me in Paradise."
Luke 23: 39-43

Moment of Silence

Story:

 Sometimes, the only thing that I can really equate to how I want my relationship with God to be is to think of it kind of like a solar system He's the sun and everything revolves around his life and what he has done for us... from there, I imagine the rest of the universe trickling out to all those people whose lives, He has touched and the colder, more distant planets and milky ways that have yet to come across this source of life, and need to be told by those who do know; to start a wave by telling all the people around you, you know? And then they tell the people around them and so on, until the word has touched all of those little planets and stars that no one really thought it would ever make a difference, whether they were exposed to it or not.... Everyone counts

Moment of Silence

All: Father I ask that you stay at the center of my life. I ask that you guide me through my day and be with me every step of the way. Give me strength and help me to overcome the obstacles that are placed before me with the help of thy word and thy grace. Watch over us,keep us in thy safe keeping ,keep us free from the clutches of the adversary. deliver us from evil and forgive us when we fall short. Help us to do thy will..

Station 12: Jesus Speaks to His Mother and the Disciple

Leader: We adore you, oh Christ, and we bless you.
All: **Because by your holy cross you have redeemed the world.**

Reading:

Standing by the cross of Jesus were his mother and his mother's sister, Mary the wife of Clopas, and Mary of Magdala. When Jesus saw his mother and the disciple there whom he loved, he said to his mother, "Woman, behold, your son." Then he said to the disciple, "Behold, your mother." And from that hour the disciple took her into his home.
John 19: 25-27

Moment of Silence

Story:

DOORS

Look back and thank God.

Look forward and trust God.

Look around and serve God.

Look within and find God.

God closes doors no man can open and

God opens doors no man can close.

Moment of Silence

All: Father I ask that you stay at the center of my life. I ask that you guide me through my day and be with me every step of the way. Give me strength and help me to overcome the obstacles that are placed before me with the help of thy word and thy grace. Watch over us,keep us in thy safe keeping ,keep us free from the clutches of the adversary. deliver us from evil and forgive us when we fall short. Help us to do thy will..

Station 13: Jesus Dies on the Cross

Leader: We adore you, oh Christ, and we bless you.
All: **Because by your holy cross you have redeemed the world.**

Reading:

It was now about noon and darkness came over the whole land until three in the afternoon because of an eclipse of the sun. Then the veil of the temple was torn down the middle. Jesus cried out in a loud voice, "Father, into your hands I commend my spirit"; and when he had said this he breathed his last.
Luke 23: 44-46

Moment of Silence

Story:

I am not a religious person at all, but very spiritual I believe in god and I go to him all the time, in prayer. I mediate because that's where I find my connection...i feel right know i want to be so close to him but I don't want to contradict my self. I want to love god with my all, but theirs so many things in my life that don't follow gods word.. and I don't want to disappoint... I want to always be on track and I feel like I'm off right know... One day hopefully when I get myself together I will grow to have that strong connection with god.. and i wont have to go back on anything i pray or do...

Moment of Silence

All: Father I ask that you stay at the center of my life. I ask that you guide me through my day and be with me every step of the way. Give me strength and help me to overcome the obstacles that are placed before me with the help of thy word and thy grace. Watch over us,keep us in thy safe keeping ,keep us free from the clutches of the adversary. deliver us from evil and forgive us when we fall short. Help us to do thy will..

Station 14: Jesus is Placed in the Tomb

Leader: We adore you, oh Christ, and we bless you.
All: **Because by your holy cross you have redeemed the world.**

Reading:

When it was evening, there came a rich man from Arimathea named Joseph, who was himself a disciple of Jesus. He went to Pilate and asked for the body of Jesus; then Pilate ordered it to be handed over. Taking the body, Joseph wrapped it [in] clean linen and laid it in his new tomb that he had hewn in the rock. Then he rolled a huge stone across the entrance to the tomb and departed. *Matthew 27: 57-60*

Moment of Silence

Story:

In The Center Of God's Will
By Herbert Buffum

In the center of God's will I'm sweetly resting,

And I know that naught can harm me anywhere;

As a mother folds her arms about her children,

So I'm safely kept in Jesus' loving care.

In the center of God's will I'm safely hiding,

And no evil can befall me where I dwell;

'Tis the secret place known only to God's Children,

Oh, the peace that fills me now no tongue can tell.

In the center of God's will I am contented,

Tho' the clouds at times my hide His loving face;

I am kept each day by His almighty power,

And I'm resting in His all-sufficient grace.

In the center of God's will, why should I murmur?

For I know that in His loving Fatherhood,

He'll permit no evil thing to overtake me,

And "all things" shall work together for my good.

In the center of God's will, oh, what a refuge!

I will hide me til the storms are past;

In the center of His will He'll ever keep me,

Til I see His precious face at last.

Moment of Silence

All: Father I ask that you stay at the center of my life. I ask that you guide me through my day and be with me every step of the way. Give me strength and help me to overcome the obstacles that are placed before me with the help of thy word and thy grace. Watch over us,keep us in thy safe keeping ,keep us free from the clutches of the adversary. deliver us from evil and forgive us when we fall short. Help us to do thy will..

The Lord's Prayer

Our Father, which art in heaven,
Hallowed be thy Name.
Thy Kingdom come.
Thy will be done on earth,
As it is in heaven.
Give us this day our daily bread.
And forgive us our trespasses,
As we forgive them that trespass against us.
And lead us not into temptation,
But deliver us from evil.
For thine is the kingdom,
The power, and the glory,
For ever and ever.
Amen.

The Apostles' Creed

I believe in God, the Father Almighty,
the Maker of heaven and earth,
and in Jesus Christ, His only Son, our Lord:

Who was conceived by the Holy Ghost,
born of the virgin Mary,
suffered under Pontius Pilate,
was crucified, dead, and buried;

He descended into hell.

The third day He arose again from the dead;

He ascended into heaven,
and sitteth on the right hand of God the Father Almighty;
from thence he shall come to judge the quick and the dead.

I believe in the Holy Ghost;
the holy catholic church;
the communion of saints;
the forgiveness of sins;
the resurrection of the body;
and the life everlasting.

Amen.

Made in the USA
Charleston, SC
30 January 2012